Ladder of Shadows

The publisher gratefully acknowledges the generous contribution to this book provided by the Ahmanson Foundation Humanities Endowment Fund of the University of California Press Foundation.

Ladder of Shadows

Reflecting on Medieval Vestige
in Provence and Languedoc

Gustaf Sobin

Foreword by Michael Ignatieff

UNIVERSITY OF CALIFORNIA PRESS

Berkeley   Los Angeles   London

University of California Press, one of the most distinguished
university presses in the United States, enriches lives around
the world by advancing scholarship in the humanities, social
sciences, and natural sciences. Its activities are supported by
the UC Press Foundation and by philanthropic contributions
from individuals and institutions. For more information, visit
www.ucpress.edu.

University of California Press
Berkeley and Los Angeles, California

University of California Press, Ltd.
London, England

Library of Congress Cataloging-in-Publication Data

Sobin, Gustaf.
   Ladder of shadows : reflecting on medieval vestige in
Provence and Languedoc / Gustaf Sobin ; foreword by
Michael Ignatieff.
      p.   cm. — (An Ahmanson Foundation book in the
humanities)
   Includes bibliographical references and index.
   ISBN 978-0-520-25334-6 (cloth : alk. paper) —
   ISBN 978-0-520-25335-3 (pbk : alk. paper)
   1. France, Southern—Antiquities.   2. Archaeology and
history—France, Southern.   3. France, Southern—
Civilization.   I. Title.
   DC607.4.S659   2009
   944'.802—dc22   2007052242

Manufactured in the United States of America

18   17   16   15   14   13   12   11   10   09
10   9   8   7   6   5   4   3   2   1

The paper used in this publication meets the minimum
requirements of ANSI/NISO Z39.48-1992 (R 1997) (*Permanence
of Paper*).

CONTENTS

FOREWORD

Michael Ignatieff

Ladder of Shadows is an interconnected meditation on the history of Provence from the decline of the Roman Empire to the birth of Romanesque Christian civilization a thousand years later. It is a story of collapse and destruction, rebirth and renewal. It is the story of how Europe was reborn from the Dark Ages. It is also a study of how mosaics and sarcophagi, statues and pillars—the fragments of art left behind—reflect and transmit the experience of a civilization's collapse and rebirth.

The narrative is told as a tale of fragments. Sometimes the fragment is a light blue shard of glass the author found on the site of a seventh-century glassworks. From this tiny fragment an essay re-creates the vanished world of itinerant glassworkers. Sometimes the fragment is a torso of Venus, the statue's arms, legs, and head severed a thousand years ago, we discover, by early Christians determined to obliterate these threats to the flesh-denying severity of their new faith. Sometimes the essay tells the story of a whole building, a forgotten Romanesque chapel high in the hills of northern Provence. We learn that such chapels were the work of itinerant Lombard stonemasons, illiterate craftsmen who first perfected the architecture of the vaulted stone roof and, in doing so, heralded the dawn of a new age.

These fragments are woven together, essay by essay, into an ensemble that readers will interpret and enjoy in different ways. For some, this will be a book about the tenacity of human survival in a time of barbarian invasion, cultural collapse, and economic disintegration. For others, the essays will strike a lighter note, as a loving travelogue through a Provence most tourist itineraries would ignore. Scholarly readers will read this text as a study of how generations of historians, archeologists, archivists, and restorers have preserved and deciphered the fragments that tell us the story of Europe's painful rebirth. I am sure the author wanted the book to be read in these and other ways. But he surely wanted it understood on a spiritual level as well. *Ladder of Shadows* is a book about the longing of a vanished society for transcendence; for escape from the mortal confines of fear, hunger, and death; for a message of validation from the godly and angelic world beyond. This is a book about the search for salvation, for hope, for belief, in the thousand years of loss that swept Mediterranean Europe after the collapse of the Roman Empire. In our own time of violence and disenchantment, the author believed, this vanished past, painstakingly reassembled from shattered fragments, offers us a warning and an example.

Ladder of Shadows is steeped in the work of scholarship, but its author was not a scholar. He was a poet, and his ladder of shadows was built, rung by rung, over forty years wandering the terrain of Provence, searching for traces of the past. It is a ladder of images and ideas that enables the reader to step down into the depths of time, to the deepest roots of our culture, to the buried foundations and barely visible mosaics in which the most profound meaning of our heritage is to be found.

Gustaf Sobin was a friend of mine for over thirty years. Born in 1935 in Boston, he graduated from Brown University and lived for a time in Cambridge, Massachusetts, struggling to become a writer. With a deep love of French poetry—particularly the works of Saint-John Perse and René Char—he moved to France at the age of twenty-six. I remember him recalling, with a happy sigh, his first drive from Paris to Provence. It was René Char's influence that drew him southward; Char, a powerful poet and one of the chief organizers of the Resistance in the Vaucluse, lived in l'Isle-sur-la-Sorgue. Sobin came to sit at his feet and learn the craft of poetry; the two were to become close friends.

Sobin bought a small stone house in a hamlet in the Vaucluse. The hillside behind it was covered it with oak, and its front windows looked out over vineyards, stone-girded terraces, and peach and apple orchards in the valley between two beautiful medieval hilltop villages. Dominating the view, though fully visible only on clear days, stood Mount Ventoux, fifty miles away, its white stony upper elevations giving it the appearance of being topped with snow all year round.

Beside Sobin's house stood a large *borie*, over two meters high, an igloo-like structure of fieldstone, with a low entrance and a conical vault inside. These structures, some dating back to Neolithic times, once dotted the fields and upper pastures of Provence. They were built to shelter shepherds and flocks, to store tools and grain. No doubt the *borie*, a mysterious symbol of ancient peasant skill and ingenuity, was part of what drew him to the house, as well as its isolation. He must also have chosen the place because everywhere there were sources of inspiration: barely two hundred yards away the tiny chapel of Saint-Véran, one of those Romanesque chapels he memorializes in this book; ten miles toward Roussillon, the Gallo-Roman Pont-Julien, a sturdy Roman bridge still taking traffic across the Coulon River nineteen hundred years after Roman engineers had thrown its delicate triple arch over the rocky gorge. From every vantage point, too, Sobin would have seen Mount Ventoux, associated forever with the memory of the Italian medieval poet Petrarch, who had made a historic ascent of the mountain in the fourteenth century, leaving behind an ecstatic letter describing his exploit. It was Petrarch too who had installed himself at Fontaine-de-Vaucluse, twenty miles from Sobin's house, to write the famous sonnets to Laura that reinvented the classical humanist tradition of lyric love poetry, a tradition Sobin himself was to follow. In his new home, he knew he had found the point of convergence of the poetic, archeological, and cultural inspirations necessary for his work.

At first he lived alone in two stone rooms, the living quarters upstairs and a small, book-lined study in the basement, where he would sit next to the furnace to write. In the late 1960s he met Susanna Bott, an English artist who was painting in a studio in Lacoste. After they married and had two children, the couple built an addition at the back, with rooms for the children, a sitting room, and a kitchen. In the early 1970s Sobin built a *cabanon*, a single whitewashed room with a large window facing the valley. For the next thirty-five years, except for breaks to travel, he would wake in the dark, eat breakfast, and walk the two hundred yards to the *cabanon*, where he would remain until noon, writing. No computer ever found its way into the *cabanon*. He would write first with a pencil in his ornate, laborious, oddly childlike but legible script, and then transcribe good versions with his Mont Blanc fountain pen. Afterward he would have a simple lunch in the kitchen, often alone, and then return to the *cabanon* for revisions, corrections, and typing. He typed on a portable Olivetti that he kept functioning for thirty years as the world around him went digital. In the evenings he would read, at first fiction and poetry but then, increasingly, the historical and archeological studies that inform his essays. Over the first ten years he wrote solely lyric poetry, later turning his hand to novels as well. One of his five novels, *The Fly-Truffler*, earned him his first widespread commercial and critical recognition. Finally, he also became an essayist of a unique kind: writing poetic meditations on the archeology and art of Provence. His first collection, *Luminous Debris*, published in 1999, covers the prehistoric to Gallo-Roman periods. *Ladder of Shadows*, its companion volume, continues these explorations through the Middle Ages. The intensely wrought, elliptical, and stylized quality of Sobin's essays cannot be understood apart from his work as a poet and novelist. The essays are unique in their display of a poet's gift for imagery in rhythm and a novelist's instinct for narrative.

I first walked up the long winding track to Gustaf's house on Christmas in 1972. I was living in my family's summer house in a nearby village, and a mutual friend had suggested that I meet him. The man who came out of his study to greet me was a tall, stooping figure, wearing a pair of corduroy trousers, a denim *bleu de travail*, and sturdy Paraboot walking shoes. His black hair was swept back from his forehead, and he had a drooping black moustache. His eyelashes were thick behind wire-rim glasses. His voice was soft, sometimes bordering on the inaudible, and he spoke with a gentle, meticulous expression, his English already sprinkled with Gallicized words. His manners were courtly, absentminded, and extraordinarily gracious. We talked in his study for hours, drinking *vin ordinaire* out of cups. Lit by his study lamp, the walls of the room were lined with bound volumes of Joyce, Faulkner, Hemingway, and French poets. I was struck by how beautiful the editions were; this was clearly the library of someone who loved books as objects. On the shelves above his writing desk were arrowheads, shards of Roman roof tile or medieval pottery, found on his walks in the fields. As he talked he would pick up one of these found objects and turn it over in his hand. Above the study desk, pinned on the bottom shelf at eye-level, was a small slip of paper bearing words in the wobbly hand of his son, Gabriel: "*je suis le roi.*" I am the king.

The uncompromising quality of Sobin's life, the smallness of the little stone house, the cold darkness of the Provençal winter all around, the bitter starry night, the hard light on the white table where he worked: all of this was very romantic to me. It was clear he had spent a decade trying to master the craft of lyric poetry, waiting for the angels to descend, alone out there in that freezing *cabanon*. At that time there was nothing to show for it either—a publication or two in an American university review, but otherwise piles of rejection letters, and no reaction from readers—nothing but the accumulation within him of a slowly building sense of confidence in his own talent, fed and sustained all on its own. I'll never forget the exhilaration I felt as I walked back down the hillside in the cold starry Provençal night after our first meeting, feeling that I had met a man who had made a radical and courageous choice in his way of life. We became immediate friends and remained so for the rest of his life.

It was an intermittent friendship. Sometimes a year would go by and I wouldn't see Gustaf, yet when I walked up the path to his house, he would embrace me and kiss me on both cheeks, and we would pick up as if we had never parted: drinking *vin ordinaire*, talking, and sometimes just sitting together in companionable silence on the terrace by the *borie*, watching night fall on the valley. He dedicated some of his poetry to me, including some touching verses about the flowering of the almond trees in February, the month my son was born. But I cannot say I understood the abstract, fevered lyricism of his work. He didn't care whether I did or not. In his quiet way, he was one of the most stubborn, dedicated, and intransigent artistic personalities I've ever met. In time, we talked less about poetry and writing in general, perhaps sensing that it was better for our friendship if we left literature aside. Over time, too, I came to realize that much as I admired him and his life, his path was not for me.

Recognition finally came in the 1980s, following a visit from the renowned American poetry editor James Laughlin, whose celebrated press, New Directions, would publish three of Sobin's books. Once Sobin's poetry had received Laughlin's imprimatur, young poets and editors of reviews and anthologies began making the trek up the hill to his *cabanon*. Gustaf was pleased—confirmed—but he had lived so long without recognition that he no longer needed it.

I remember best our walks together. In the late afternoons, when he had finished working and it was cooler, he and I would set off to visit a Romanesque chapel, a Roman ruin, or a Neolithic dolmen—a huge rock shaped like an excised tooth, standing in the middle of some sloping glade and mutely begging us to explain how it had got there. Gustaf would share his knowledge; he was already talking to the local archeologists in Avignon and Aix, taking out books from the local library, and digging deeper into the multilayered past beneath our feet. Once he took me up the Gorges de Veroncle, a deep cleft in two templates of rock between Gordes and Roussillon, through which a vigorous torrent once rushed. We climbed into this strange gorge, almost hidden from the sun, grown over with vegetation, ever more enclosed in the steep, once water-washed but now bone-dry canyon walls. The feeling, Gustaf remarked, was obstetrical, as if we were struggling our way back up some gigantic birth canal, away from birth and back toward conception. At the root of the gorge, as if by magic, the ruins of an early modern water mill appeared, the giant millstones bound by hoops of iron still intact though covered with foliage. He eagerly pointed out the canals that peasant masons had dug to channel the water through the paddles, now rotted away, though their iron frames hung limply over one of the mill races.

All his walks had wonders in store like this. Many of the places he took me to—the monastery at Gagnagobie, the stout country-side chapel of Saint Gabriel with its lamb of God over the entrance door—figure in *Ladder of Shadows*. He was a singularly attentive walker, all senses tuned and on alert. He would stand stock-still in some orchard, as if listening to a sound far away, and then dig the toe of his shoe into the dirt between the rooted vines and turn up a glistening object which, when he had bent down, picked it up, and rubbed it clean with his thumb, turned out to be an arrowhead. Walking with him, you were never just there, in the surface of the present. You were always conscious of walking on buried layers of the past visible if one only slowed one's pace, bending as he did to pick up the vanished traces. The previous collection of his essays, *Luminous Debris*, gave us the first results of these thirty years of walks through the countryside of Provence.

His direction was always the same, away from the familiar to the unknown: away from the cars, the tourists, and the signposted promenades, and off into the *garigue*, the thyme- and rosemary-scented hillsides of shale and gorse, following goat and sheep paths, thinking aloud, sometimes with a guidebook, sometimes a cadastral map, seeking the traces of the vanished past.

Every tourist visits the Pont du Gard, the astounding three-tiered aqueduct built by Roman engineers over the rock pools of the Gard River near Nîmes. For a thousand years, fools and lovers have cut their names into the massive stone pillars of its base. Sobin walked away from all that, to the obscure traces of the Roman irrigation system that fed the aqueduct as it cut through the countryside between Arles and Nîmes. Over many years, he explored the traces of the Roman water canals in garden walls, olive groves, and oak woods, and from these findings he produced one of his greatest essays. It is not on the aqueduct in its century of glory, when it fed the Gallo-Roman town of Nîmes and all the rich farms in between, but when the barbarians had sacked everything, when the discipline and order of the empire collapsed and everyone began siphoning water off the aqueduct, which quickly dried it up and rendered it useless. This fascination—not with the moment of glory but with the moment of destruction and loss—runs through *Ladder of Shadows* as a sustained note of melancholy.

The same note of melancholy came to dominate our late afternoon walks in the 1990s. A constant theme of our conversations was the touristic despoliation—as he saw it—occurring all around him. A wave of change swept over his Provence just as both he and I arrived there. The Provence I remember from 1962 was dry and deserted: fields abandoned by families whose sons had been drawn into the towns by the economic boom; villages deserted because they were too damp and windy in the winter, while young families now preferred suburban villas with a garden and central heating. This Provence was an artifact of the Fourth Republic, where you waited in line all morning to make a long-distance phone call at the post office; where old men in bleu de travail played *boules* in the village square and then cycled home un-steadily on old two-wheelers; donkeys were heard braying in the fields, still pulling wagons piled with stone or forage; and many of the old *mas*, the stone farmhouses in the fields, were boarded up and empty because the families had moved to the towns.

Then came the real estate boom, fuelled by the commercial glorification, by magazine editors, real estate agents and other promoters, of a Provençal lifestyle of red-tiled farmhouses, ele-gant dining under vine trellises, and smoky late afternoon views over olive groves singing with the sound of cicadas. The *mas* were sold to real estate speculators. Old shutters were pried open and revarnished in strange, new, non-Provençal colors. The red tiles on the floors were polished; holes were punched through old stone walls and French doors were put in to admit the light; swimming pools were sunk in vineyards; hilltop villages, aban-doned for years, now boasted top-quality hotels and spas; smart art galleries opened in village *caves*; Souleiado prints and post-cards sold at every village *épicerie*. The boom brought employ-ment to an army of masons, electricians, painters, swimming pool contractors, cooks, and housekeepers, while farmers' markets set up at the crossroads on Sundays, crowded with smart Europeans as well as superbly dressed Parisians, now able to commute down for the weekends on the fast train, the TGV. Suburban *lotissements* were built throughout the valley to hold the new population that flocked in to enjoy the new jobs and the southern lifestyle. Villas of ever-increasing size and splendor dotted the hillsides, changing the landscape forever.

Gustaf lived right at the epicenter of this economic revolution, and it appalled him. Peasants were being enticed off their land by unscrupulous real estate speculators; the dignified and restrained architecture of peasant France was being looted by the *nouveaux riches*. The rugged old *mas* were now being turned into smart, gated spas and hotels. The agricultural base of a whole civilization was going under, with more and more families selling out their vineyards, olive groves, and stone *mas*, because the prices offered them beat anything they could make by staying on.

We argued over the meaning of these changes. He saw a new form of barbarian invasion—I do not exaggerate—while I saw new life coming back to old villages. He saw local families being convulsed by the temptations of greed. I saw families making a good living. The people I employed as I rebuilt my family's house, and yes, put in a pool too, seemed to benefit from it as much as I did. But where I saw change and growth, he saw a spreading vulgarity and cheapness of spirit.

I see now, as I look at *Ladder of Shadows* and reread *Luminous Debris*, how deeply his disenchantment with modernity ran, how central it was to his nature and to his work. I wish we hadn't argued. There was no real point, on my part, in defending the suburban gardens and villas that were, from his point of view, desecrating the landscape. Desecration was the issue, not protecting his own privileges. He was not a snob. He didn't want to deny anyone the pleasures of a house or a garden of their own. But he felt, with increasing passion, that Western society had taken a wrong turn, tearing down and building over the past, ignoring the spiritual resources and consolations that it offered, in favor of a present-minded, appetite-centered modernity that glutted our hungers but ultimately left them unsatisfied. Much of this metaphysic of disillusion courses through *Ladder of Shadows*. It will help readers to understand this metaphysic if they remember that while he was writing these essays, Sobin felt the beloved ground being ripped out from under his feet.

In reaction to the changes sweeping away the world he loved, he turned his back on the present and spent more time in museums and archives; in ruins, deserted chapels, and dank caves where hoarded coins were once discovered; in fields where vestiges of ancient street and house plans could still be discerned; and in dark churches where restorers were struggling—millimeter by millimeter, wielding trowels and pincers, applying solvents with cotton wool—to save thousand-year-old mosaics from vanishing. *Ladder of Shadows* is the result of this turning away from a gloomy present to an impalpable but precious past. No book I have read is a more touching homage to these humble scholars who rescue the past from the wastage of time and the contemptuous forgetting of contemporary generations.

Yet *Ladder of Shadows*, like the work of the heroic restorers it celebrates, is a triumph over its own pessimism. No book, indeed, is a more ringing refutation of its own melancholy. While every page decries loss, erosion, effacement, vandalism, and disappearance, every page is also a patient demonstration, by a great writer, of what writing can do to save, preserve, and redeem.

Consider one example: the essay on the medieval glassblowers. All that remains of their work more than fifteen hundred years later are tiny rounded shards in the dust, all but invisible to the naked eye, stirred to the surface only by Gustaf's own tenacious attentiveness at a place called Sainte-Marthe. As he says, glassblowers

are close to a poet's heart. Like the glassblower, the poet fuses disparate substances together by "an abrupt increase in temperature—
be it caloric or intellectual"—and then infuses them with breath to
create an object of pure transparency. As the glassblower breathes
out, the glass is blown. As the poet exhales, the word comes forth.
And then, as he stands amidst the tiny speckles of glassblower remains in a field at Sainte-Marthe, he remarks,

> As for ourselves, as we gain control or—what amounts to ex-
> actly the same thing—lose control over our own ecosystem,
> it's hard to think that the future won't depend on how we
> read—examine—vestiges such as this. Won't depend, for in-
> stance, on how we come to interpret four hundred years of
> virtual silence that left us—at Sainte-Marthe at least—with
> little or nothing if not its tears. Its blue tears. The long pen-
> dulous waste of its blue translucent tears.

In conjuring the image of the glassblower and the poet, Sobin
manages an act of resurrection and redemption. These forgotten
glassblowers, now so vanished there is not even a trace of their
bones, are immortalized by an act of remembrance, and their
tears, the sorrow of a whole forgotten epoch, are not forgotten.

This writer did not succumb to melancholy or misanthropy,
did not let the pessimism that darkened his life take away his faith
in his own task as a writer, which is to remember, to save, and to
redeem. I do believe, as his friend of thirty-five years, that you
hold in your hand his finest achievement.

On my last visit with Gustaf, in the summer of 2004, we sat on
the terrace and talked as old friends do, not having to finish sen-
tences or identify who we were talking about, since we both knew.
We remarked how strange it was that we had grown old together.
Our children were adults now. I had remarried and had returned

to teach at Harvard. He had lived to see some real recognition for his work: favorable reviews, appreciative features in the *New York Times*, translations in several languages, even that bauble of success, a movie option on one of the novels. All of it amused him, and none of it seemed essential. He was not distant, but he was ever more detached.

He announced that he was completing the inventory of his archive: his manuscripts, his correspondence with literary figures like René Char, all of it meticulously kept and filed, and now being patiently identified by number and described in an inventory intended for sale. He was working at it with his daughter, Esther. It made sense to sell the archive to a university (it now belongs to the Beinecke Library at Yale).

Late in the autumn of 2004, Sobin was diagnosed with cancer. He died at home, with his family around him, on July 7, 2005. On a burning July afternoon, dozens of his friends and his family gathered for his burial service at the village cemetery in Goult. Words were said and blown out of hearing by a dry Provençal wind. My wife and I laid a pebble each on the vault and walked away hand in hand. The vault was the barest and most unadorned concrete. A year later, when we visited the grave again, we discovered the vault had been covered with sheets of stone that took the afternoon light and reflected it back softly. Onto the stone, Gustaf's sculptor son, Gabriel, had carved a half dozen beautifully spare sheaves of wheat, a bas-relief whose classical simplicity, whose loving evocation of the Roman sarcophagi father and son had often visited together, would have given Gustaf deep pleasure.

> *Michael Ignatieff is a Canadian Member of*
> *Parliament, a writer, historian, and journalist*

INTRODUCTION

Ladder of Shadows is about matter and immateriality: about the un-abated attempt on the part of medieval societies to surmount the often dire circumstances of their day-to-day lives by the conjuration of invisible forces. In the twenty-five essays that follow, I have tried to give as much attention to one as to the other; as much, that is, to the underlying conditions of those societies, as to what-ever traces—be they iconographic, architectural, or sacramental—testify to that incessant, seemingly inherent, appeal. The former, of course, prefigures the latter; the circumstantial, the supplica-tory. It's only out of so much rubble, bone heap, and shattered glassware that, on occasion, there appears evidence of that ascen-sional constant, that imperious, if ephemeral, invocation. Only, indeed, on rungs of shadow will it—under certain conditions—come to manifest itself.

As a companion volume to *Luminous Debris*, a collection of es-says touching on the prehistoric, protohistoric, and classical his-tory of Provence and Languedoc, *Ladder of Shadows* picks up where the former left off: with late antiquity. In approaching the medieval, it seemed to me necessary to prepare the terrain, even if summarily, for what ensued. For it might be said that the *textus* of the medieval is due as much to the warp of classicism as to the weft of Christianity. Each will weave its way—inextricably— through the other to produce a fabric that we'll come to recognize, ultimately, as that of Europe in a nascent state.

As in *Luminous Debris*, each essay in the present volume arises out of an examination of some particular aspect—often, some evocative detail—chosen for the light it might shed on a far larger field: that of the existential itself. Be it bits of late Roman coinage, the mutilated torso of some marble Venus, the blue debris of an early medieval glassworks, or the powder rasped from the reputed tomb of Mary Magdalene, each instance serves to illustrate not only its own moment in history but the attempt—however hallucinatory—to transcend that very history and, so doing, surmount an otherwise irremediable fate. Throughout the thousand years that the present study touches upon, there seemed to be no greater need on the part of medieval societies than that, indeed, of the transfigurative; than the quest—by the intermediary of bone, splinter, or effigy—of a dimension *past themselves*.

In concentrating upon a particular area such as Provence and Languedoc within a given framework of time (roughly the third to thirteenth centuries), one is struck by both the wealth of readily available materials—be they vestigial or archival—and the susceptibility of those materials to wear, erosion, effacement. An inscription, for instance, on the limestone impost of a Romanesque chapel at Mirabeau in the Vaucluse, celebrating a solar eclipse on the third of June 1239, has nearly vanished in the last twenty-five years under the abrasive effect of an unremitting mistral. Another Romanesque edifice, Saint-Christophe-de-Vachères (Alpes-de-Haute-Provence), collapsed altogether when a sonic boom, emanating from a passing aircraft, brought down its stone slab roof. Nothing, though, is more susceptible to effacement than fresco. Subject to any number of natural agencies, not to mention deliberate depredation on the part of invaders or religious dissenters, the fresco—no thicker than an eggshell—has often vanished, leaving little more, say, than some documentary account of how, in a long-abandoned church (Lasplanques [Tarn]), a Mary once floated between the cusps of a crescent moon.

Today we're confronted by a new, far more insidious, form of effacement. Given the immense wealth of computerized information readily available at the tip of our fingers, we're all too likely to confound the virtual with the veritable: the *descriptive*, transmitted electronically, with the *described*, pertaining as it might, say, to some inimitable historical artifact. Endowed with volume, texture, and patina, the testimonial presence of such an artifact doesn't lend itself to *re-presentation*. Its "aura" (*dixit* Walter Benjamin) doesn't replicate. Within a remarkably brief period of time, however, our entire field of perception has radically shifted. Far too often, for example, such artifacts will find themselves divested of their own most tangible properties, and reduced to little more than a ribbon of electronically processed data. Drawn out of all original context, deprived of every contingent factor, they exist no longer as palpable quantities unto themselves but as empty vessels, gutted of each and every attribute for the sake of some digital abstract.

History, however, is something—ideally—we'd touch. It's something that begs approach, examination, appraisal, in relation to its own underlying properties. For only in entering into direct contact with whatever vestige history has left us can we begin to apprehend not only the veritable conditions of a given epoch but the numinous climate in which it surrounded itself.

If any of the essays that follow brings the reader a bit closer to such an appreciation, the present volume—based on on-site investigations of medieval vestige in southeastern France—will have fulfilled its own, albeit limited, ambitions.

❧

Apt

Reading an Antique City as Palimpsest

Lying buried like some deep, richly endowed level of human consciousness, the vaulted cellars and subterranean passageways of an antique city often preserve the memory of an otherwise obliterated existence. Such is the case with Apt. Roman to its roots, medieval to modern in its every outward manifestation, Apt exists in an inherent dichotomy of its own. The modern city as if floats—perfectly oblivious—over the antique. Indeed, much of the city's population, today, is scarcely aware that just beneath the level of its bakeries and newsstands, its workshops and toolsheds, lie the eloquent voids of another age, another civilization. One can walk down the Rue Sainte-Anne, for instance, passing on one side Céramique Viguier, Coiffeur Élisabeth, Boucherie Gaudin without for a moment realizing that one is walking down the full length of a Roman forum that will end, 140 meters later, with the Établissement Montagard (*plomberie, sanitaire, chauffage*) and the Pompes Funèbres Amic. Beneath these small shops and services run, in vaulted chambers, the substructures of what was once the very center of all Roman public life. In fact, throughout the heart of the city these substructures—be they readily accessible at the base of medieval stairways or hopelessly confounded within the dense urban magma—preserve the original plan (call it the "skeletal outlines") of this lost Roman colony, *Apta Julia Vulgientium.*

I'd have to ask myself, however, why I found Apt more evocative of classicism than cities within the immediate area endowed with far richer monuments. Why, that is, these cellars "spoke" in a way that the great oval amphitheaters of Arles and Nîmes or the windblown colonnades in the excavated ruins of Vaison-la-Romaine simply didn't. Why, in short, as the trace grows fainter, the vestige—following the inverse logic, say, of homeopathic pharmacology—grows more and more poignant.

Quite clearly, the city was laid out according to a rigorous, pre-established plan. Typical of Roman urbanism, this plan, gridlike in character, imposed a network of streets running either parallel or perpendicular one to the next. First of these streets, the *decumanus maximus,* founded upon an east-west axis, served as the city's main thoroughfare. This, in turn, was intersected at right angles by the *cardo maximus,* running north to south. The intersection of these two streets (Rue des Marchands and Rue Sainte-Delphine in the case of present-day Apt) served as the city's center (today the nondescript Place du Postel). Within this rigorously geometric program, specific areas were assigned for the various public monuments, such as the forum and basilica, the theater and the city baths. If, with time, a certain urban development far less formal in nature extended past the city itself, there is little or nothing *intra muros* that doesn't testify, today, to that original, originating act: the city pre-conceived as a single, inseparable, organic entity.

Apta means very much what it suggests: apt, suitable, well dis-posed. This might have originally referred to its harmonious com-position as a city or, perhaps, its strategic position along the *Via Domitia*, the all-important transalpine trade route between Italy and Gaul. Indeed, the *Via Domitia* once ran clear through the heart of the city, forming as it did a section of the aforementioned *decumanus maximus*. As to its second nominative, *Julia* suggests that the city was founded at either the time of Caesar or that of Augustus at the outset of his reign: before, that is, 27 B.C.[1] Lastly, *Vulgientium* draws its origin from the name of an indigenous Celtic tribe, the Vulgientes, whom the Romans had come to sub-due and, in the process, "Romanize." Indeed, the very reason for establishing the colony of Apt altogether, situated as it was be-tween the pacified plains below and the still hostile hinterlands beyond, lay in Rome's need to consolidate the region as an inte-gral part of its empire. *Vulgientium* served, undoubtedly, as an in-vitation to that indigenous population to enter into its protec-torate. For Rome as a colonizing power didn't merely subjugate; it drew, seduced, integrated the innumerable tribes of Gaul into its ever-expanding realm.

One has, then, enough material evidence from the given ves-tiges themselves and enough documentation beginning with Pliny the Elder to reconstitute the general outlines, at least, of this lost city. A recently discovered cellar, here; an embedded section of fluted column, there; the blue *tesserae* of a once sumptuous mosaic floor, yet there again: all testify for that long-vanished colony. Oth-erwise one would be hard pressed, today, standing in the midst of the Apt marketplace on a bright Saturday morning, to believe that such a world ever existed. That such an underworld *still did exist.* Caught in the wafted odors of flowers and diesel fuel, the shouts of fishmongers and rag-dealers, it would be hard to believe, indeed, in any world but one's own, any moment in time but that—all too precarious—in which one stood.

The past draws. It draws, I feel, to the extent that the present, the cultural and ultimately the spiritual present, has failed to generate generative image: the kind in which societies might come to recognize their veritable identity. In default of such image—such eloquent mirror—one turns backward. Goes under. For certainly one is never searching for anything except oneself. Be it among the blown detrital particles of some vanished galaxy or the thrashing tails of some microscopic protozoan, one is always in search of the kind of phenomena that might, potentially, confer sense upon one's own existence. This is especially true, of course, with the cultural. Never do those inherent identities find fuller expression than in the glissando of an aria, the floating gaze of a saint on some pitted fresco, than—yes—in these choked cellars, blind corridors, the interrupted running of so much finely molded plinth. Curiously enough, the relative inaccessibility of these *caves* only adds to their attraction. Against the cultural poverty of one's own times, it seems befitting, I feel, to travel under. Examine vestige. Explore the subterranean chambers of an antique city as if they constituted, as suggested, some deep, richly endowed level of human consciousness.

One soon realizes, however, that in such cities one is confronted by *two* histories: that of its construction and development, then that of its effacement. If I'd grown somewhat familiar with the former (I'd read all the relevant documentation, traced the outlines of the city's monuments with the aid of historic survey maps, and visited every accessible cellar), I gradually realized that this second history—dealing with the antique city's obliteration—was every bit as informative as the first. If the city's construction and development read like a single uninterrupted lesson in logic, civic order, and imperial glorification spanning a full five centuries in time, its second history expressed itself in one sporadic, destructive event after another. This second history would come to a close ten centuries later in the deliberate dismantling of whatever vestiges still remained of that once radiant colony.

Apt, if anything, is a palimpsest. One need only enter its households, peer just beneath its tufted carpets and richly waxed ceramic tiles, and examine its vaulted substructures, below, to draw such an analogy. For there, one quickly comes to recognize not only the "text" itself but the innumerable layers of its effacement. Of that effacement, there seem to have been four distinct factors or agencies at work. Two of those agencies might be considered strictly natural. Water, as one of them, repeatedly came to flood the city. Lying alongside a river, Apt has traditionally been subject to violent, unpredictable inundations. Each would leave an unmistakable deposit of sand and gravel, still visible today in the excavated cross sections of certain subterranean chambers (e.g., the cellar of the Musée Archéologique). One may safely assume that in a time of efficient public administration such as that of the Roman Empire, these alluvial deposits were immediately removed by maintenance workers. Following the collapse of the Empire in the fifth century, however, they were left— apparently—to accumulate. Today, as part of the archeological record, they lie concentrated in stratigraphic ribbons of various widths, testimony to that historic abandon.[2]

A far greater factor of effacement would be soil erosion: what seeped, bit by bit, into the city from the facing hillsides to the south. Often called colluvium, these deposits took on dramatic proportions. Given that the Roman city, according to modern historians, was more or less flat, it's astonishing to find today that the ground level of its buildings differs in depth from an average of four meters in the heart of the city (the theater, basilica, and capitol) to as much as ten meters to the south (the southern extremities of the forum). If alluvial river deposits never amounted to more than forty centimeters, these aggradations that invaded the city from the surrounding hillsides accounted for all the rest.

Several hypotheses have been advanced for this phenomenon. It's quite possible that Apt, in expanding, began terracing those hillsides for the sake of both garden cultivation and house construction. The disrupted topsoil then began trickling downward—slowly, inexorably—in the direction of the city. Here again, one can be assured that during the Empire this colluvium was removed at the very same rate it accumulated. With the Empire's collapse, however, one is left—once again—with an image of unmitigated disorder, desolation. Apt as a functioning civic entity no longer existed. Suffering from the first waves of barbaric invasions, it had already entered—within a brief period of time—the Dark Ages.

One historian attributes the marked difference in depth between the colluvial deposits in the southern part of the antique city and those at the center to the presence of ramparts.[3] These ramparts might well have served as a buffer throughout the early Middle Ages. Rather than invading the heart of the city, the colluvium simply collected, bit by bit, against their exterior facades. This is still apparent, today, in the sudden difference in elevation (the *dénivellement*) of certain buildings that once abutted those very structures. Another historian suggests the possibility that Apt was abandoned altogether toward the end of the sixth century.[4] Its inhabitants, fleeing the successive invasions of Lombards and Saxons, sought refuge in perched sites within the immediate area. The desertion of Apt might well have lasted as long as two centuries, time enough for an entire section of the city to vanish under the mass of so much uninhibited sedimentation.

Of all the agencies of effacement, none left a trace thinner yet more incriminating than fire. It is the very signature of the invasions. "Between the Lower Empire and the end of the tenth century," writes Guy Barruol, "there is archeological and documentary evidence (*Cartulaire d'Apt*) that the city underwent, at least partially, five separate destructions."[5] A thin carbonaceous layer (the result of some violent conflagration) will lie directly beneath a thicker, looser stratification composed of gray ash, scorched iron, and charred ceramic. These "documents," as the archeologists call them, speak for themselves. If Apt escaped the first precocious waves of Germanic invasions (255–270), it certainly fell prey to the Burgundians (456–457), the Visigoths (470), and, soon after that, the Franks. This would be followed by the Lombards and Saxons (569–575), and a period of such obscurity that only the ruins, the rubble, the calcinated deposits would be left to testify for history itself. The last wave of invasions—that of the Saracens—Moorish tribesmen emerging out of Spain— "destroyed everything that the Lombards and Saxons somehow managed to spare."[6] Their sporadic raiding parties would reduce the city to near ruins for two successive centuries, most notably in 725, 730, and 869. Here again, only the rubble would be left to testify; only the cinder, to speak.

One may safely say, then, that the lost Roman city of Apt underwent obliteration by water (river flooding), by earth (soil erosion), and by fire (the result of five successive centuries of vandalization). The remaining element, air, can't be held responsible for any such effacement except, perhaps, as a passive quantity. For it's the vestigial remainders of those Roman monuments—lying out in full view—that became the object, in late antiquity, of a particular form of public appropriation. If those monuments had already undergone partial destruction at the hands of invaders, far more were deliberately dismantled by the inhabitants themselves. The stones were needed—and urgently—for reassembling the city's defense system. A second rampart, constructed out of whatever stones were near at hand, came to surround a so-called "reduced city." Apt had begun shrinking, withering about its center like some degenerated organ. As a bastion of *romanité*, the end was near.

Throughout Gaul, Roman monuments were being converted into quarries, into open-air warehouses of readily available building materials. The magnificent edifices of one culture were reemerging as the hastily assembled keeps, watchtowers, bulwarks of another. Apt would be no exception. It had begun squatting in the midst of its own past, borrowing here, pilfering there, improvising everywhere. A vision of the provisional—the makeshift—had come to replace that of the everlasting. The dismantling of antique monuments would continue, what's more, well past the Dark Ages. In fact, once western Europe had emerged out of that ponderous obscurity, dressing itself—as Radulfus Glaber once put it—"in a white gown of churches," the process of demolition would not only continue but accelerate. For those immediately available materials were needed for that vast program of reconstruction we've come to call the Romanesque. The twelfth-century cathedral of Apt would literally rise out of both the substructures of a Roman basilica, just beneath, and the hewn blocks, columns, architraves of the Roman theater lying immediately alongside. As the cathedral expanded between the fourteenth and seventeenth centuries, that adjoining Roman theater would steadily, inexorably vanish. "Les chrétiens sappèrent l'amphithéâtre," one contemporary exclaimed.[7] Now, as the city entered the Renaissance, excavating its subsoils for the sake of fresh constructions, more and more vestige came to light. In 1685 Marmet de Valcroissant would remark: "Every day, more or less everywhere in Apt, one finds columns, figurines, tombs in marble, some perfectly plain, others richly inscribed and decorated."[8] In 1780, another observer, Abbé Giffon, would marvel at the remainders of a Roman bath *(thermae)* recently unearthed behind the present-day Sous-Préfecture. Along with the baths were discovered fragments of a sculpture, a bas-relief depicting a woman sodomized by a donkey, and no less than twelve marble-lined dressing rooms.[9] As for the last standing antique monuments, they would vanish from sight altogether in 1870. Until that date, many of the massive stone tiers of the Roman theater had remained visible, as had parts of the stage itself. So, too, had an immense stone archway and a series of arcades in the present-day Place Carnot.

All in all, it had taken medieval-to-modern Apt a millennium and a half to bury its antique counterpart. Across that vast expanse of time, the "text," gradually, had been relegated to "subtext"; the founding vision, to that of suppressed recollection. Indeed, in working my way through all the relevant documentation or, quite simply, exploring the city, I've often asked myself whether I hadn't inadvertently fallen onto a metaphor for civilization itself. For here, in this urban palimpsest, all the elements for such a metaphor can readily be found, be it in the antique city's edification or in its ensuing demolition. Isn't it this, this metaphor, finally, that draws, attracts? Far more than the monuments per se, isn't it the successive strata, the compilations inherent to history that intrigue? They are similar in so many ways to our own psychic composition; one is always drawn to some suppressed level of intent: the long embedded trace, say, of some instigating vision. Uninhibited, here, by the monuments themselves, by fluted columns and massive entablatures, one willingly goes under. Apt, in this sense, is privileged by default. Yes, one willingly goes under, especially now, in the "aging of the world"—in the *mundus senescit*—peering into each of those vaulted, subterranean chambers as if a certain lost promise, therein, lay waiting.

Desolate Treasure

Treasure hoards serve as an index of sorts to the violence of
human history.

Aline Rousselle

Bronze coins, dating from late antiquity, still occasionally come
trickling out of the mouths of caves, grottoes, rock overhangs.
Worn, often obliterated, they're found only a few meters from the
very places in which—nearly two thousand years earlier—they'd
been hastily buried. Scarcely bigger than chickpeas and no thicker,
for the most part, than the head of a thumbtack, they bear singular witness to a violent moment in human history. They
constitute—one comes to learn—the scattered remains of some
personal treasure, buried against the first waves of barbaric invasion that would decimate, eventually, all of Gaul, setting its cities
ablaze and laying low its countrysides.[1]

The coins aren't dated, but they bear both the name and the effigy of the emperor reigning during the period in which they'd
been issued. They thus provide specialists with an infallible grid

for making chronological attributions. All too often, the last minted coin emanating from a particular cache will correspond— within only a few years—to a specific wave of invasion. One comes to indicate the other: the artifact, product of a high if sclerotic civilization, will coincide in time with the very agencies of the civilization's effacement, what would leave—as memento— little more than smoke, rubble, and the charred expanse of an unending series of grain fields.

Strange, one thinks, how something so small, so seemingly insignificant, could testify for such a decisive moment in the course of history. For there, at that precise time (260–280), one Germanic tribe after another would invade the essentially stable, homogenous world of the Gallo-Roman: what had enjoyed—for nearly three hundred years running—the immense benefits of the *Pax Romana*. Strange, too, one thinks, standing before the entry to one such grotto, situated high over the pellucid green waters of the Gardon, that those invasions were caused by pressures— environmental and, in turn, socioeconomic—originating at a distance of over eight thousand kilometers from the grotto itself. One learns, for instance, that these invasions, in Jacques Le Goff's words, "were probably only the consequence of some initial impulse that might have arisen out of a profound change in climate, a drop in temperature from Siberia to Scandinavia that would reduce the pasturelands and arable grounds of these barbarous populations, and—one pushing the other—send them migrating both to the west and to the south."[2] Out of the steppes of central Asia, the Huns, themselves pursued by the Ogoures, and the Ogoures by the distant Sabires, forced the relatively sedentary German tribes (be they those of the steppes, the forest, or the coastline) to migrate—in turn—westward, aggressing, pillaging, decimating as they went. Across two full continents, an inexorable chain reaction, affecting one tribal society after another and ultimately the entire Roman Empire, had been set into motion. It would determine the shape and character of the Western world—and indelibly so—from that moment forth.

Until then, the Romans could consider the world neatly divided between that of the civilized and that of the barbarous. The frontier, or *limes*, running between the two defined the outer limits of the one and the burgeoning periphery of the other. "To reflect on the nature of the *limes*," wrote Yvon Thébert, "is, in fact, to reflect on the nature of the Roman Empire altogether: one conditioned the other."[3] Monolithic, this seemingly impervious, self-enclosed megastructure defined itself as a totality. Enveloped in the epidermis of its frontiers, it self-sufficed. When, however, those frontiers began to weaken, yielding at certain strategic points along both the Danube and the Rhine to the pressure of Germanic tribes, who were themselves pressed from behind by "those both stronger and more merciless," it underwent fracture.[4] At first, the barbarous invasions were little more than raids, pillaging parties, motivated more for the sake of booty, spoliation, than for the acquisition of land. The first invaders came to plunder, not settle. Toward the end of the fourth century, however, the Huns, in crossing the Don—displacing as they went one Germanic tribe after another from their homeland—drove those tribes by *force majeure* into the heartlands of the Empire. There, in response to such an onslaught, the Empire underwent a process of cellulation. Its populations fell back into relatively secure circumscriptions while abandoning large areas to their invaders. Alemanni, Franks, Vandals, and Visigoths poured into those "interstitial zones," establishing themselves—often on a permanent basis—in the midst of an empire that had shattered into a plethora of iso-lated parts.[5] By the middle of the fifth century, it would disintegrate—as if dissolve—altogether. If Europe, a European identity, would emerge eventually out of a fusion of those warring factions, so totally opposed by nature, it would take a full seven hundred years of misery, famine, and internecine struggle for it to do so.

Here, though, in inspecting the numerous little grottoes that pock the rock abutments along either side of the Gardon, it's the very first wave of those massive migratory displacements that draws, intrigues. It would send the local Gallo-Roman popula-tions scampering into whatever remote shelters they could find for themselves. For weeks if not months, whole families would hover in these damp inhospitable cavities, having buried—upon arrival—their meager savings for safety's sake. If, today, archeol-ogists happen to unearth a monetary hoard buried in any one of those innumerable grottoes or, quite fortuitously, a single coin comes tumbling forth, one can fairly well assume that its previous owner suffered a tragic end. "Each hoard which was not recov-ered, and which has therefore come down to us . . . represents a genuine misfortune for its former owner, a catastrophe which, in many cases, he may well not himself have survived."[6]

Uberitas reads one such coin, depicting the figure of Abun-dance, a cornucopia cupped in one arm, a sheath of wheat grasped in the other. *Uberitas*, indeed. It's not the coin itself, however—somewhat worn and relatively common to the numis-matics of late antiquity—that draws all one's attention, but the coin contextualized: placed, that is, within the unraveling fabric of history. Suddenly, this desolate treasure—the pathetic residue of an all-traumatizing event—comes into perspective. So doing, it finds itself released from its quality as isolated object—historic curio—and can assume, henceforth, its rightful place within the continuum. Isn't this true, indeed, for all artifact? All vestige? The real meaning of particulars can only be found, ultimately, within the throw of the incessant. Seen in such a manner—one determined by the ongoing pulsations of an historic dynamic—these thin metallic slivers not only enlighten; they tend, occasionally, to glow.

Crypto-Christianity

The Sarcophagi of Arles, I

While the Gallo-Roman countryside found itself repeatedly ravished by barbaric invasion from the third century onward, cities such as Arles remained relatively unscathed, having hastily surrounded themselves in ramparts, watchtowers, fortifications. As a bastion of late antiquity, Arles not only resisted, it continued to flourish as an epicenter of socioeconomic and cultural activity. This "little Rome," as it was often called, became the emperor's part-time residence at the outset of the fourth century and began minting its own money soon after, before being named—by 418—the praetorian prefecture of all Gaul. In the midst of its bustling malls, public baths, and civic basilica, it thrived as a rich provincial metropolis. "Within its walls," Honorius would proudly declare, "can be found each and every treasure of the Orient."[1] Among the many imports reaching Arles from the East at this time (silks, perfumes, gold-threaded brocades) came, in fact, something far more precious. Whether in the form of spoken rumor or that of the earliest evangelical texts inscribed on bands of papyrus, there came the first covert promises of the new faith.

Curiously enough, though, those promises—like a luxury product in themselves—reached, first of all, the sensibilities of the most privileged stratum of Arlesian society. Unlike in Rome, it wasn't the *humiliores* who embraced that long-awaited message of redemption from the outset, but a class of patricians, languishing in the late light of Roman antiquity. They, too, would have been the first in Gaul to conform to a new praxis in regard to burial. From the reign of Hadrian onward, rather than cremate their kinsfolk, they interred them within richly decorated marble sarcophagi. It's these very sarcophagi, entirely pagan at first, that allow one to trace the slow yet irrepressible diffusion of that long-awaited message as it came to manifest itself in one elaborately carved panel after another, converting so much rumor, whisper, surreptitious text into resplendent marble.

"This new disposition," writes Henri-Irénée Marrou, "arriving as it did *pianissimo* in the first century, emerged progressively, defining itself in the third century and becoming all-dominant under the Late Empire in the fifth."[2] Indeed, the inherent drift in such a transformation, moving from a classic to Christian idiom, is—in iconographic terms—often imperceptible at first. One would have to examine meticulously, for instance, a sarcophagus such as that of "The Olive Harvest" (*L'olivaison*) in the Musée de l'Arles Antique to discern the slightest difference (fig. 1). Reading its fragmented frontal panel from left to right (as intended, that is), one discerns a tree full of *putti*, naked aside from their broad, wind-buffeted capes. Propped upon ladders, they're plucking olives off the tree's branches. Eminently idyllic, the entire panel celebrates a traditional bucolic scene from Mediterranean classicism. Nothing

Figure 1. Sarcophagus of the olive harvest (detail). Musée de l'Arles et de la Provence Antiques. Photo by the author.

therein appears to announce the all-critical transformation. While other *putti* at the base of the tree pour their harvest into heavy wickerwork baskets, several more haul those baskets to an olive press immediately to the right, manned by a matching pair of fellow juvenescent laborers. It's only there, finally, in carefully inspecting the vertical axis that rises up from the olive press, that one comes to discern the occluded fact. Virtually hidden in the dense foliage of an overhanging olive bough, a tiny bar in raised relief bisects—at right angles—the vertical axis of the olive press. Together, bar and axis describe—one discovers—an altogether hermetic cross.

Even if the sarcophagus dates from the period of Constantine's conversion and the ensuing peace with the Church (early fourth century), it serves to illustrate the languor with which this privileged class—deeply imbued with the decorous splendor of late Roman antiquity—gave graphic expression to their newfound faith. Fervor, here, was still subject to the prototypes of a certain preestablished iconography. In this period of so-called crypto-Christianity, Gaulish neophytes, unlike their Roman coreligionists a full century earlier, weren't so much intent on hiding their faith as finding an adequate scenography for its expression. During that transitional period, however, the nascent theology would remain remarkably discreet. One might even speculate that the olive as evangelical symbol lay disguised in so much ambient classicism at a time when its consecrated oils had come to be considered an unction in the service of baptism and "a beneficent and healing substance when . . . in contact with relics."[3] For the moment, however, the liturgical remained safely concealed within the bucolic.

Yet another early Christian sarcophagus, also housed in the elegant galleries of the Musée de l'Arles Antique, displays a similar penchant for pagan decor. This sarcophagus, that of "The Dioscuri," was executed, however, nearly a full century later: at a time of massive conversions and a thoroughly established, fully accepted, diocese within the city proper. Its reminiscent character, then, becomes all the more astonishing. Set in a classic architectural motif of four successive porticoes, the sarcophagus depicts, in the second and third of those porticoes, the betrothal of a young couple followed—many years later—by their death and separation. The elapsed time between these two scenes is suggested by the physiological changes that each has undergone in the intervening period: the bride's body, in the latter panel, has grown stouter, more matronly, whereas her smooth-cheeked bridegroom appears bearded with an altogether world-weary expression upon his face. If the bride tenderly grazes the shoulder of her spouse in the first of these scenes, in the second—their hands clasped—each mournfully bids the other an everlasting farewell. Resolutely pagan, these matching portraits are flanked, furthermore, by the presence of the Dioscuri. Naked, both Castor and Pollux—reined horses in hand—occupy, in fact, the first and fourth porticoes of this four-part architectonic program. As Greco-Roman psychopomps, they symbolically serve to assure the deceased couple a safe journey across the Lethean wastelands and unto the Blessed Isles of the Everlasting.

One would have to examine the side panels of this sarcophagus, however, to determine its veritable theological nature. For it's only there, in scenographic retreat, that this stone coffin declares its evangelical message. While one side panel portrays Christ in the miraculous act of multiplying the loaves and fishes, the other depicts Peter as disseminator of the faith. Paul-Albert Février has suggested that these side panels, markedly different in both expression and execution from the frontal section, might have been the work of another sculptor at perhaps an entirely different moment.[4] Be that as it may, the entire work displays the ease with which a certain senatorial class, at this particular time, could move from the classic to the Christian as if across a single, unbroken continuum.

As the last and perhaps most resilient example of lingering pagan iconography in the midst of the new all-pervasive theology, one might consider—in passing—the figure of the *orante*. Commonly depicted on the reverse side of Roman coinage, this representation of *Pietas*—her face raised skyward and her arms spread, palms up, in reverence—will enter the new faith without undergoing any outward modification whatsoever. Graphically, she remains exactly the same. Semantically, however, she will have acquired an entirely new status. No longer the emblematic figure of civic (and thus imperial) acquittance, she comes to personify the soul in a resolute state of devotion. As the *anima innocenti* of a nascent Christianity, she will appear depicted in catacomb frescoes more frequently than any figure but that of Christ himself. There, arms raised, palms lifted, she'll embody the description repeatedly given in the Scriptures, such as that in the hundred-and-forty-first Psalm: "Let my prayer be like incense duly set before thee / and my raised hands like the evening sacrifice."

Significantly enough, she will often appear in these subterranean frescoes standing in the midst of a pastoral decor, surrounded by doves, peacocks, and—most especially—grazing sheep. Often, too, she'll be portrayed in the immediate vicinity of yet a second pastoral figure: that of the Good Shepherd. In the garb of a common pagan herdsman, nothing, at first, distinguishes this image of Christ from that of its antique prototype, Hermes Kriophoros: he who warded off the plague by carrying a ram upon his shoulders about the city walls of Tanagra. As savior figures in a pastoral milieu, one can easily be confounded with the other throughout this critical period of crypto-Christianity. However, as Henri Leclercq has written, "the Good Shepherd of the catacombs—young, svelte, beardless—has come to replace the

Greek divinity whom, in physical beauty, he so much resembles."[5] Under the guise, now, of the classic, emerges the Christian. And, as it does, a curious association develops between *orante* and shepherd: between, that is, the hieratic figure of the adorer and the object of her adoration. Call it "syncretism," "juxtaposition," or "mystic affinity," one accompanies the other more and more frequently as Christian iconography rises up out of the catacombs, and, in moving from the pictorial to the plastic, increasingly expresses itself in the bas-reliefs that adorn the earliest Christian sarcophagi.

Granted, the *orante* will occasionally appear in the form of an *orant*. Representing, for instance, the soul of a dead man, the personification of *anima* (intrinsically female) will assume, under the circumstances, male characteristics. Then, too, figures from the Old Testament, especially Noah, Abraham, Isaac, and Daniel, will often be portrayed as *orants*, their arms raised heavenward in that selfsame gesture of divine adoration. The presence of the male *orant*, however, usually excludes that of the shepherd, whereas the presence of the *orante* almost invariably draws, induces, provokes that of her male counterpart. Immobile, as if frozen in epiphany, all of the actors in this metaphysical drama repeatedly appear in the earliest Christian bas-reliefs in close if not immediate proximity. Over and over, they seem to coexist in a state of mutual solicitude (fig. 2). The distance between them, however, tends to expand as the pastoral milieu in which they first emerged finds itself gradually replaced by that of the biblical. With the outset of the fourth century, this tendency will have grown irreversible. "Both shepherd and *orante* are relegated, now, to opposite extremities of the cistern," writes Leclercq, "separated either by intervening figures or by the rhythmic whiplash of the strigil motif."[6]

Figure 2.   Good Shepherd and *Orante*. Musée de l'Arles et
de la Provence Antiques. Photo by the author.

The shepherd, henceforth, will appear as Savior, and the Savior, soon after, in the triumphant role of *traditio legis*, the dispenser of divine instruction. As for the *orante*, she'll disappear altogether by the end of the fourth century, replaced by a plethora of devout female figures, drawn directly from the Scriptures and readily identifiable, now, by an evangelized public. Indeed, within a very short period of time, iconography—be it pictorial or plastic—will have moved from one of quiet pastoral allusion to one of direct pedagogical statement. A clandestine faith, in the meanwhile, would have grown into something not merely public but pervasive, all-dominant.

Today, in inspecting sarcophagi such as those depicting agrarian *putti*, the psychopomps Castor and Pollux, or the *orante* in her sublimated rapport with the Good Shepherd, one is witness, in fact, to an idyllic if short-lived moment in the transmission of cultures. It is as if the nascent faith hadn't fully detached itself as yet from the opulent twilight of Roman antiquity; as if, indeed, they both, momentarily, had managed to coalesce, enjoying—if for no more than that moment—a sublime instance of inherent inseparability.

Terra Sigillata

Once again, one finds oneself reading the ground, scanning the earth's surface for some residual trace, some fortuitous sign. If, in the furrows of a recently plowed wheat field, one happens upon scattered bits of gray ceramic, stamped occasionally with a distinct geometric pattern, one might well be reading early Christian artifact. Called "DS.P" by the specialists (sigillata-derived early Christian pottery), this slipware—local in facture and dating from the fourth to fifth century—constitutes a "text" unto itself. In consulting the appropriate documentation, one learns, for instance, that this particular ceramic marked an altogether abrupt departure from that of its traditional Gallo-Roman predecessor in terms of its form, its impressed decor, its paste, and its glaze.[1] Rustic, even "barbarous," according to specialists, it reflects that critical moment of transition in late antiquity in which an exhausted culture gave way to the gathering fervor of a new faith. It marks, in short, the arrival of the *tempora christiana*.

In considering decor alone, one has gone from that of Roman antiquity, richly charged with raised figuration, to a redundant set of highly stylized, emblematic motifs. Within a single century, characterized by invasion from without and the penultimate signs of a military, administrative, and economic breakdown from within, scenes celebrating classical mythology vanish altogether. Be it Venus and her entourage of winged cupids or Bacchus wreathed, stout, and cavorting, the dramatis personae of the pagan world disappear forever. So, too, those figures that had endeared themselves to the Gaulish public: the hunter, the circus acrobat, the gladiator. It's as if history, like some kind of wind disseminating so many semantic particles, had blown into the deepest recesses of human consciousness an entirely fresh set of cognitive signals. These signals would appear, now, stamped—sigillated—upon the pottery. Torsades, palm fronds, arches and archways, not to mention the wheeling disk of rounds and rosettes, find themselves imprinted in a seemingly inexhaustible variation on the thoroughly predetermined. Here, manifestly, one graphic vocabulary has come to replace another.

Not only decor but technique undergoes a radical transformation at this time. The rich molded relief of imperial slipware—what allowed its personae to swell in contour, assuming an evocative presence against the high mirrorlike gloss of one ceramic vessel after another—vanishes as well. Instead, the motif goes under, finds itself impressed in the yet-unfired clay. The "message" conveyed by this fourth-century pottery no longer exults in the celebration of earthly pleasures. Embedded rather than embossed, it grows hermetic—codified—in the somber gray matrix of an emergent common ware.

Simultaneously, the quality of the finished work undergoes an equivalent transformation. Within a short period of time, it degenerates into something rustic, markedly artisanal, "handmade." From the exquisite, technologically perfected craftsmanship of Gallo-Roman antiquity—exemplified by the workshops at Graufesenque (Millau, Aveyron), in which 450 recognized potters produced signed works for a vast clientele spread throughout the better part of the Roman Empire—to the tiny workshops producing "DS.P" in the fourth century, the *ars cretaria* has clearly suffered an irreversible decline. What, indeed, did happen in the interim? If that elegant red-glazed ware with its "sharp, glass-like facture" reached its apogee under Hadrian in the second century, by the third century the conditions necessary for such a production—a stable economy, a large available workforce, and an inviolable network of communication throughout the entire Empire—could no longer be assured.[2] Reflecting those very conditions, the pottery henceforth is no longer signed. Its paste grows coarse and its overall execution, markedly careless. The molds, used over and over, aren't recast, now, but reemployed to a point of total obliteration. What's more, for the first time, the clayware produced in Provence is reduced-fired (as opposed to oxidated), a process far more complex in itself but affording an immense economy in wood fuel. One may safely assume from this conversion that wood, its availability, the workforce necessary for its provision, and a road system secure enough for its transport have suffered default as well. By the end of the third century, the molded red slipware that once celebrated—in all its pagan splendor—the collective mythologies of the Roman Empire has been totally replaced by its rustic successor.

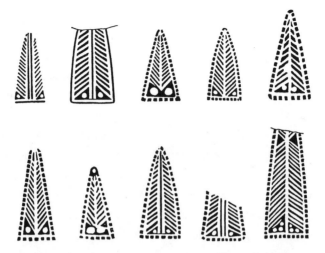

Figure 3. The ubiquitous palm frond. Drawing courtesy of Jacqueline and Yves Rigoir.

At first, the pottery emanating out of these successor workshops bears little or no decor whatsoever if not an occasional guilloche. It's characterized at the outset by its austerity. Gradually, though, it adopts the grammar of ceramic imports that have just begun entering Gaul from north Africa: from the evangelized and politically stable regions of *Africa proconsularis*. This table- and cookware abounds in impressed geometric motif. Wheels, festoons, arches and archways, as well as the ubiquitous palm frond, embellish the cups, bowls, plates, and tureens of this imported ware (fig. 3). Soon, workshops in southern Gaul would adopt much of this geometric grammar themselves. That grammar, one comes to learn, had already traveled an extensive distance before reaching the shores of southern Gaul. If the ceramic produce originated for the most part in Tunisian workshops (directly to

the south of ports such as Marseille and Arles), the grammar
it disseminated arose, centuries earlier, out of cradle civilizations
located in the Near East. From there, it made its way across the
northern rim of Africa, transiting through Luxor, Fayum, and
the Nile Delta to Tunisian centers of production such as Carthage
and Hadrumetum. By way of example, one need only consider the
palm, palm frond, or palmette motif. Eminently oriental both as
a plant (most specifically that of the date palm) and as a signifier,
it came to represent in Mesopotamian cultures a highly stylized
tree of life, a heart in its reception of the sacred, or—upon
occasion—the emblem of sacredness itself. For the Egyptians,
"the palm leaf, worn on the head or held in the hand, was an attribute of the god Heh, the personification of eternity."[3] Later, in
early Christian iconography, it would represent the promise of
everlasting salvation as epitomized by the palm of Palm Sunday.
The sign, embedded within the ceramic, would reach southern
Gaul, finally, at the end of this immensely long peregrination.
There, in the hands of local potters, it would quickly become an
integral part of their hermetic grammar of redemption.

If history, as already suggested, might be compared to a wind, that
wind—in this particular instance—arose out of the east. It blew
across the entire expanse of the Mediterranean, bringing with it the
particles of a fresh semiotics. At the same moment that Syrian
merchants were discharging wine from Gaza, papyrus and cotton
from Egypt, and spices from Persia, this very wind—all the more
powerful for being impalpable—had begun disseminating, in Henri
Focillon's words, "the dreams, both abstract and fulgurous, of the

desert monks."[4] For a society diminished by successive invasions, by the first devastating waves of plague, and by a general economic and administrative breakdown, these "dreams," celebrating an *elsewhere* as far removed as possible from their own rampant distress, could only have been deeply welcomed.

Within a remarkably short period of time, one iconographic vocabulary would have replaced another. Far more determinant for Western civilization, however, the abstract sign—as the basic unit of this new, profoundly static semiology—had come to replace figurative representation within the human *imaginaire* (see "Venus Disfigured," p. 44 below). Henceforth, the sign would no longer reflect a given reality, but suggest—intimate—yet another. It would point, now, rather than portray; imply rather than depict. Toward a world deferred, *par visibilia ad invisibilia* in Saint Paul's words (Romans 1:20), it would—in its own hermetic manner—show the "way." In this diacritical displacement of the senses, a "codified conception of the universe that not only dismisses the representation of the human figure but treats it with disdain, tending to envelope and denature that representation in the play of its meanders," would monopolize all forms of graphic expression.[5] The sign, functioning as promissory signifier, be it embedded in clay or carved in shallow relief across countless sacramental panels, would serve to determine human consciousness for the next six hundred years—until, that is, the advent of the Romanesque.

Relics

Membra Martyrum *as Living Current*

> The cult of martyrs may have been the most significant
> element in the religious life of the fourth century.
>
> Henri-Irénée Marrou

More than any other single factor, it was the scattered bones of its
earliest martyrs—the tibiae, clavicles, skull plates—that brought
life to the nascent faith. Enveloped, quite often, in rich brocades,
these skeletal sections, invested with a numinous existence, came
to sanctify the first basilicas. Indeed, the least oratory, chapel, or
ecclesia required, for its consecration, some such *membra martyrum*. How, though, one might ask, could such a pathetic memento, often spurious in nature, serve to vivify that very faith,
abolishing as it did the barriers between the "here" and "hereafter," thus allowing—in Saint Victricius's words—"the eyes of
the heart to open"?[1]

Martyrdom and, in turn, the cult of martyrs emerged in the midst of a fading Roman Empire. Within an historical context, it developed as the Empire collapsed. Upon the close of the Severan dynasty (193–235), instability from within and the encroachment of barbarian successor states from without undermined the little that remained of a once assured, if sclerotic, order. Despite Constantine's conversion and the ensuing peace with the Church that put an end to the persecution of Christians, the *memoria* of the earliest martyrs took on ever-increasing significance in the popular imagination. For the Roman subject had begun looking *elsewhere*. Rumors of an ultimate form of salvation had begun circulating throughout the Empire, generated by the exemplary lives—and, far more, the exemplary deaths—of those reputed to have attained such salvation. If anything, those earliest martyrs showed "the way." Intent upon imitating the Passion of Christ, they underwent what contemporaries called "baptism by blood." In abnegating their earthly condition, they willingly submitted to a death that could only be considered transfigurative. At the end of an instant's agony, they felt assured that an everlasting glory awaited them.

In reading hagiographic accounts today, one is repeatedly struck by the eagerness those early martyrs displayed in gaining access to that glorious state. One can even detect, occasionally, a voluptuousness at play in their very precipitation. Saint Victricius, for example, describes how a woman, "avid for death, incited the wrath of a lion by rubbing herself against its flanks; another, in denying her own child milk, entered the arena with her breasts full, flaunting them before a pack of rapacious animals; yet another, a virgin, aglow with all the jewels of eternity, offered, for necklace, her very neck to the executioner."[2]

Immediately after such public scenes of sacrifice, early Christians were quick to gather up whatever little remained of those venerable figures. Often, only the "hardest parts" actually remained: those (as described in the *Martyrium Ignatii*) that hadn't been devoured by the famished animals. At Tarragona, after the martyrdom of Saint Fructueux, the devout stealthfully entered the arena well after nightfall to amass his relics. Not only had the saint's body, they discovered, been devoured by wild beasts, but whatever remained of his bones had been set ablaze. Reverently, the devout poured wine over the martyr's still fuming pyre, then carried off his charred parts to a clandestine site for the sake of their veneration.

The Roman authorities were quick to recognize the power and—potentially—the subversive magic invested in such relics by the early Christians. Now they not only burned the martyrs' bones but, as in Lyon in 177, flung their ashes into the eddies of some fast-flowing current: there, that is, where even the *memoria* of such martyrdom might be forever dissipated. The Christians, in response, took to increasingly covert methods to preserve anything that might remain of that most precious of substances. For the relics spelled access. "Anyone who touches the bones of martyrs," wrote Saint Basil, "is partaking in the holiness and grace that resides in them."[3] Given that martyrs served as intermediaries with the divine, possession of their least, seemingly inconsequential, osseous section afforded the parishioner a privileged means of address. Vectorial by nature, relics functioned as instruments of approach in communicating with the godhead. (See "Mary Magdalene the Odoriferous," p. 184 below.)

Not all martyrs, however, underwent dismemberment and dispersion at their death. Early Christian history is filled with resonant, if often apocryphal, accounts of clandestine burials. "According to Gallic sources, martyrs' tombs were frequently invisible. They could only be detected by the toponyms that their mere presence had generated, for during the period of persecutions every measure was taken to dissimulate their remains in order to avoid disinterment and dispersion at the hands of their persecutors."[4] It wasn't only the toponyms, however, that marked their presence but—according to hagiographic reports—nature itself. "Over the *sepulcrum* of Baudilius at Nîmes," reads one, "sprang a laurel; in the orchard at Embrun where the remains of Nazaire and Celse lay hidden, sprouted a pear tree; at Brioude, next to the tomb of Julien, roses—each November—blossomed. Triumphant in their death over death, nowhere were the martyrs more present, indeed, than in their tombs."[5]

When persecutions came to an end, however, and Christianity could openly declare itself in the construction of a plethora of churches, those churches, no matter how modest, required—for their consecration—consecrated bone. Over and over, one finds written evidence that those bones (or, rarely, those bodies, as invoked in the foregoing paragraph) were considered the sine qua non of sanctity. For early congregations, the remains of a martyr—be it the least calcinated ossicle—virtually set their entire basilica aglow, endowing the structure with a supernatural luminosity of its own.

There arose, now, the problem of furnishing each and every religious edifice with its indispensable relic. In dismissing spurious hagiographic accounts, one comes to realize that an area as extensive as southeastern Gaul, for instance, could only claim three verifiable martyrs: to wit, Saint Victor of Marseille, Saint Genès of Arles, and Saint Pons of Cimiez. Even if one allows for the division and distribution of certain relics (their so-called multiplication), the "demand" for such skeletal sections far surpassed the given "supply." In response, two phenomena simultaneously emerged: the earliest pilgrimages to the Holy Land, occasioned—in part— by the search for such relics; and, in the opposite direction, a rampant traffic in *membra martyrum* to meet that ever-rising "demand." Pilgrims in the fourth century would go to any length, one learns, to acquire whatever would-be relics they could. Gregory of Tours in his *Liber in gloria martyrum* relates how a woman on pilgrimage from Gaul prayed for three consecutive years at the tomb of Saint John the Baptist in the Holy Land until she was granted—quite miraculously—his thumb as a relic.[6] She then returned with this precious member and saw it duly installed in the altar stone of her parish church. Far less spectacular in nature, accounts abound describing the rapacity or simple cunning of those earliest pilgrims. One reads, for instance, how "relics of the True Cross were so prized that in Jerusalem deacons stood guard to prevent the pilgrims who came to kiss the holy wood from biting off a sliver."[7] Along with this influx of pilgrims arose, simultaneously, a class of merchants who dealt exclusively in such sacrosanct matter. Much of it, of course, was sham, counterfeit. Given, though, the fervor prevalent at that time, it was the fervor alone— more often than not—that served to authenticate so much dubious vestige.

Now not only bones but, in default, a rich array of "representative relics" began trickling into Gaul. Anything that might have entered into contact—no matter how superficially—with a martyr became, ipso facto, venerated itself. The clothing, for instance, that Saint Cyprien wore at his martyrdom, saturated with sweat, or the linen that the devout flung about the body of the bishop of

Carthage to absorb his blood, was invested with the same magic properties as the bones themselves. And, like the bones, those bits of fabric, classified as *brandea*, underwent division, dissemination, as full-fledged relics unto themselves. Torn into ribbons, even thin precious threads, their slightest parts represented, nonetheless, the incorruptibility of the whole. Then, too, objects such as a paving stone that bore the imprint of a martyr's foot or the cobbles with which that protosaint, Saint Stephen, was lapidated were deemed *reverentia* as well. For the devout, these objects were impregnated with the martyr's *virtus*. Nothing, it seemed, was too slight if it bore witness to the witness himself: "witness" being what *martyr*, in Greek, originally signified.

One might also mention in passing those venerable objects that had entered into contact not with the martyrs directly but with their mortal remains. Stone dust, for instance, scraped from their sarcophagi or a few grams of earth gathered from their reputed burial grounds would suffice, not to mention wax from the tapers and oil from the lamps that had burnt alongside their burnished reliquaries. Nothing was considered insignificant if it spelled proximity, not even the flowers that decked the altarpieces or the threads that pilgrims—rapacious—pulled from the overhanging canopies. Clearly, it was all a question of approaching, as closely as one could, the mortal remains or memorabilia of those who, by their consummate faith, had approached—as closely as *anyone* could—the godhead itself.

Now, as the bones, the *brandea*, and the aforementioned *reverentia*—either associative or analogous by nature—entered Gaul, churches, one after another, were consecrated. Repeatedly, "the deposition of relics seems to have coincided with the creation of *ecclesia*."[8] One might even ask if the church, at this point, was

anything more than the *locus martyrum* for housing those desiccated treasures. For it's their presence alone that drew the
faithful, filled them—according to Saint Victricius—"with a joy
triumphant" *(gaudio triumphorum).*[9] As the instruments of intercession, it's they that provided the fervent with what one historian
has called a "luminous trace."[10]

Saint Ambrose, bishop of Milan, had been the first to intro-
duce relics into the church proper, violating, thereby, an ancient
Roman custom that rigorously separated the world of the living
from the resting place of the dead. Their conflation, until then,
had been severely sanctioned. Now, though, an entirely new
conception of existence had come into play: an eschatological
dimension proposing a life after death had introduced yet a third
term, and—so doing—undermined the inviolable dialectic that
had always separated the living from the dead. Henceforth, the
promise of an afterlife would incite the collective imagination,
and nowhere more so than in the tangible presence of those in-
tangible spirits: the martyrs themselves. It was the femurs,
shoulder blades, phalanges that the faithful addressed now,
praying not to God directly but to His blessed intercessors.
Given, too, that these were societies that had only recently
emerged out of deeply rooted polytheistic practices, it was natural that their avenues of approach to a single, singular godhead
be manifold.

As for the relics, they were invariably deposited either within
or immediately beneath the altar stone. The choice of such a location was ineluctable. As the natural focal point of the edifice itself and the very table upon which the Eucharist was celebrated,
the altar represented the vertical axis wherein all public worship
not only converged but ascended. Furthermore, "its importance

was underscored . . . by such architectural ornaments as ciboria [overhanging vaulted canopies supported by four columns] and chancel barriers. The use of light and incense also enhanced the altar area."[11] The relics were introduced into little alcoves, called *loculi*, that were carved into the altar stones themselves, in which they were then duly sealed; alternatively, they were stored immediately beneath in underlying crypts. The access to those low, vaulted, womblike chambers was assured by narrow passageways that were named—significantly enough—*ombilici*. What term, indeed, could more eloquently express the prevalent belief at that time that so much mortuary debris represented a precondition to life everlasting? Wrapped in brocade or enshrined within glistening reliquaries, the bones of those venerable figures bespoke—for whole populations—not death but the *dies natalis:* the day of birth, that is, before the eternal.

Today, in examining a period remarkably poor in substantiating evidence (most of the hagiographic accounts can be dismissed as apocryphal, and, in Provence, little more than a few scattered baptisteries and the outlines of several ecclesial substructures still subsist), what's most striking, perhaps, is the inseparability that seems to have existed in the collective consciousness between matter and spirit. Nowhere is that inseparability more evident than in the relics themselves. Invested with near limitless powers, bones (along with *brandea* and *reverentia*) were invoked not only in favor of some everlasting beatitude but in supplication against each and every ill on earth. As the protectors of the city in which they were venerated, for instance, they were brandished against fire, floods, and lightning. They were said to bring rain in a period of drought and to disperse plague in a time of contagion. As the *medicina* against all harm and wrongdoing, these splintered bits of human tissue had the power, within the public imagination, to avert evil (apotropaic) and to induce miracle (thaumaturgic). As palpable entities, they protected, provided, and interceded for entire populations long before faith itself came to be conceptualized in theory, ideation, and—ultimately—dogma. The bones as if spoke in the name of the parishioner. It might even be said that, for several centuries running, they channeled that parishioner's most fervent wishes. As agents of intercession, they assured an uninterrupted liaison between the "here" and the "hereafter." Profoundly venerated, the *membra martyrum* were considered nothing less than the conduit unto all mystery, and, in that sense, to death—by the bias of so many broken osteological sections—but also a prelude to life everlasting.

~❧~

Venus Disfigured

Why bother to look? One need only listen.
Bernard de Clairvaux

If in the first three centuries the new faith trickled into Gaul, touching only small elite circles of the ruling class, by the fourth century it had permeated the collective consciousness at virtually every level of society. By the end of that century, fully established as a state religion, it began erecting its first churches, baptisteries, and oratories. For building materials, it employed—quite often—whatever it could dismantle, if not simply pillage, from late classical monuments. Temples, theaters, *thermae*, became favorite targets. Often they were treated as little more than quarries for furnishing the new structures with so much indispensable *spolia*. Plinth found itself recycled as plinth, architrave as architrave. What didn't undergo such a simple and direct transposition, however, were the sculptures themselves. The very embodiment of pagan religiosity, they'd come to be loathed by

44

the early Christians. Invested with the power of the deity they represented, these effigies—decked, once, in garlands and scented with incense—discharged, for the evangelized, malefic energy. "Demonic," would be the term that Saint Martin would employ in proselytizing Gaul. Often he'd see the devil himself cunningly disguised in the carved figures of pagan deities such as Jupiter, Mercury, Venus. For the nascent faith, monotheistic by nature and profoundly transcendent in orientation, there could be but one response to so much carnal—if not licentious—representation. It had to be disfigured, eradicated, at all cost. "The undoing of paganism was not a process of gentle persuasion," as one historian has written. "The instruments of conversion were frequently axe and firebrand."[1] Incited, no doubt, by the biblical exhortation drawn from Deuteronomy 7:5 to "pull down their altars, break their sacred pillars, hack down their sacred poles and destroy their idols," early Christians set to work avenging the old faith for the sake of the new. They did so by destroying, and, in destroying, nullifying the inherent power that classic effigy still, quite clearly, exercised upon their psyche.

Be it carved in the round or in bas-relief, such effigy was subject to any one of three distinct forms of degradation. The first might be called simple recycling. Given that the rise of Christianity in Gaul coincided, grosso modo, with the earliest waves of barbaric invasion, much of that antique sculpture was reemployed as basic building material for the hasty construction of urban defense systems such as ramparts, watchtowers, and the like. Marble bas-reliefs, reduced in size to conform to the dimensions of such structures, have been discovered in modern times laid indiscriminately in the midst of so much coarse medieval masonry. At Sens, for example, panels such as one depicting Ulysses consulting the seer, Calchas, or another of Orestes being led off to sacrifice, have managed to preserve—despite such mistreatment—the memory, at least, of their antique *éclat*.

Then, too, the flat marble slabs of funerary stelae emanating out of Gallo-Roman necropolises perfectly suited the needs of those hard-pressed constructors. Given that such slabs once adorned the tombs of their pagan ancestors, they serve to indicate—as little else—the cleavage that now existed between the classical world and that of the early Christian. In a matter of no more than several generations, those venerable markers had come to be treated as little more than common filler in the construction of bulwarks against the impending invader.[2]

Yet another fate befell pagan representation. Lopping off the arms, legs, and heads of antique sculpture, early Christians fed those relatively detachable members to the heavily stoked flames of lime kilns. In an iconographic holocaust of its own, so much exquisitely modeled tendon, shoulder blade, eyelid and earlobe underwent calcination at raised temperatures for the sake of furnishing artisans with an uninterrupted supply of quicklime. This *chaux de marbre* was particularly suited for stuccowork due to its high rate of adhesion. Nothing would remain, finally, of the original sculptures but the marble torsos, far too massive to feed to the kilns. These would serve—as they still do today, in countless museums and private collections—as silent witnesses to those systematic acts of dismemberment (figs. 4 and 5).

The last, and by far most flagrant, form of sculpture mutilation can be ascribed to direct, deliberate acts of iconoclastic vindication. Pickax, sledgehammer, or crowbar in hand, early Christians went to work hacking, shattering, defacing the marbles in an attempt to divest them of their still active—still perilous—

attraction. They needed to be—in a word—disempowered. Until fairly recently, this labor of deliberate mutilation was attributed to the earliest invaders. Indeed, it epitomized their barbary. However, as Émile Mâle has remarked: "These invaders, who operated at great speed, would pillage temples, villas, rich estates, before setting them ablaze and continuing on their way. One can scarcely imagine how they might have found the time to shatter bas-reliefs, decapitate sculptures, render the effigy of Roman gods unrecognizable, and then pitch all that decimated debris into whatever well shafts they could find. Unlike the early Christians, they didn't consider such effigy to be dangerous: capable, that is, of exerting a malefic influence."[3] One need only examine the gracious Venus of Nîmes to find confirmation of the foregoing remark. It was discovered in 1873 at a depth of two meters and reconstituted by archeologists out of no fewer than 103 discrete pieces. It had not only been subject to deliberate, exacting, time-consuming mutilation, but then been buried, if not in a well, then under enough earth to neutralize its all-too-active numinous properties. Its destruction could only be the work of those who'd long since been intent on reducing the sculpture to such a state.

Well burial, river burial, swamp burial: the length to which early Christians would go to disseminate the severed sections of their handiwork speaks for itself. Pagan sculpture underwent not only mutilation but—in so many deliberately dislocated fragments—interment. This would explain why many of the most eloquent pieces of Roman sculpture have been unearthed not by archeologists, operating in an archeologically charged milieu, but—inadvertently—by workers digging ditches for some public service in a nominally peripheral area. In 1651, for instance,

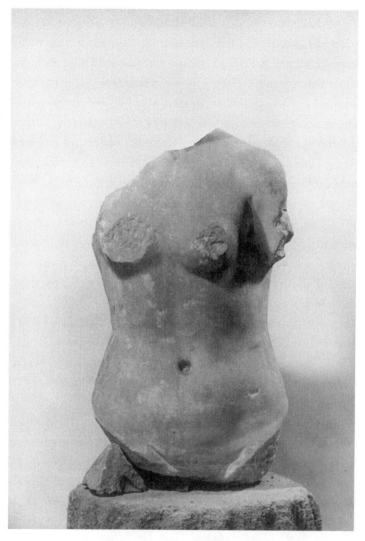

Figure 4. *The Venus of Orange*. Photo by P. Foliot, courtesy CNRS, Centre Camille Jullian, Aix-en-Provence.

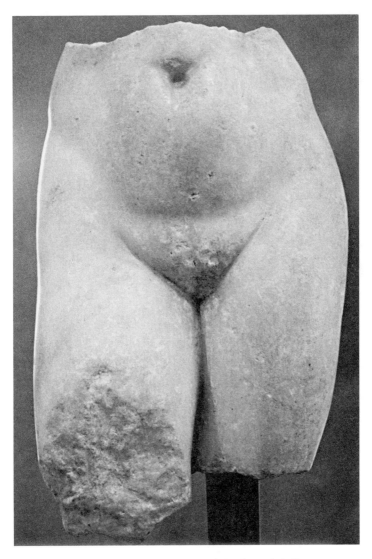

Figure 5.   Mutilated Venus figure. Musée de l'Arles et de la Provence Antiques. Photo by the author.

workers digging out an artesian well in the outskirts of Arles came upon the marble head of a woman. The beauty and heroic dimensions of this head incited them to search further. Soon enough, they discovered—in turn—her torso, her thighs, her legs, and finally the feet upon which she once stood. According to contemporary reports, only her arms were missing, that which "would put the finishing touch on her beauty" *(luy donneroient la dernière beauté).*[4]

Not all antique sculpture had the benefit of such a composite recovery. The voluptuous torso of the Venus of Orange, for instance, was discovered bereft of arms, legs, and head, while its breasts had been subject to severe mutilation (see fig. 4). Later, its head would be found as a severed section, its left eye disfigured and the entire right flank of its face neatly cleaved, no doubt, by the blow of an axe.

"By destroying cultic statues," writes Béatrice Caseau, "people were making sure that the goddesses would not have any means of harming them."[5] One might readily rephrase that statement to read: by destroying cultic statues, people were making sure that the goddesses would not have any means of charming, beguiling, abducting them—once again—into the sensuous gardens of a paganism, profoundly telluric in its orientation. It was this very magnetism to things earthen, carnal, immediate that the new faith had proscribed. It advocated, now, a marked *displacement* of the senses. A purported heaven had come to supplant a deprecated earth, and, along with it, the ever more remote figures of the venerated had replaced the corporal splendor of those decried idols. The devout had begun looking *elsewhere,* beseeching an entirely invisible deity. The murmuring spirit would replace, at this time, the idolatrous gaze as the principal vector of approach. Henceforth, the language of prayer, of liturgy, of the "word made flesh" (inverting, thus, the antique formula) would attempt to divest perception of its objects of predilection in favor of an ideology of deferment.

If Christianity adopted, at first, the iconography of late antiquity (see "Crypto-Christianity," p. 20 above), it did so only to embellish the rare sarcophagi of its elite and incise—in an increasingly abstract, geometric manner—its earliest altars, baptismal fonts, and reliquaries. From the fourth to the sixth centuries, however, even the late languishing vestiges of carved effigy would vanish almost altogether from an evangelized Gaul (see "The Deletion of Shadow," p. 59). In lieu of such effigy, the word—fervent, supplicatory, in praise of a godhead that had grown incommensurable, and thus, undepictable—came to predominate. Within a brief period of time, faith had become, for all intents and purposes, aniconic. The word could rise, now, along with the fume of tapers and the odor of incense, free of all earthly solicitations. It would only do so, however, over the hacked limbs and mutilated torsos of those deprecated idols; only do so in having suppressed each and every image of the felicitous human figure for the sake of propagating—by the bias of language—the idea of a distant, if ineluctable, state of divine remission.

The Blossoming of Numbers

The Baptistery at Riez

It's difficult to believe, today, that bathing in a river or in some natural spring could have once constituted a grave spiritual danger. As discussed, however, in "Laying the Dragon Low" (p. 76 below), certain such rivers and springs represented the last remaining enclaves of pagan mysticism in Gaul. In order to neutralize their thaumaturgic powers in the eyes of the population, the early Church issued a series of vehement anathemas, warning its congregations against the demonic forces at play wherever live water might be found. Yet hard as it tried, the Church couldn't entirely efface such a deep-seated chthonic attachment. Instead, "in order to palliate the need that had arisen from the prohibition against water sanctuaries and compensate for their loss,"[1] it came to employ a most singular means: what it couldn't fully neutralize, it channeled—in a sense, deflected. It drew the living waters out of their natural context and into a strict architectonic milieu: the baptistery. In this way, the mystery of those waters underwent a form of consignment. Enclosed within stone basins and subject to a rigid set of ceremonial observations, the waters no longer bespoke the magical powers inherent within the earth's entrails but the blessings emanating out of a remote—celestial—source. It was no longer the "here" that the waters celebrated but the promise of an everlasting "hereafter."

It should be noted, however, that baptisteries didn't begin to appear in the West until the fourth century. Prior to that, baptisms were usually performed "outdoors, after the example of Jesus's baptism in the Jordan and other baptisms described in the Book of Acts (8:36–38; 16:13–15). Justin Martyr described initiates as simply being led 'to a place where there is water' (I *Apol.* 61). The *Didache* recommended running water, although if it was not available, any water would do (7.1–2). Tertullian insisted that 'it makes no matter whether one is washed in the sea or in a pond, a river or a fountain, a cistern or a tub' (*De baptismo* 4)."[2] One can readily assume, then, that the earliest Christians treated living water with much the same reverence as did their pagan contemporaries. For the first three centuries, at least, water didn't need to be tapped, cloistered, as if disassociated from its telluric origins. It still belonged to the third day of Creation: as an inseparable part, that is, of an earth divinely conceived.

What happened, then, between the time of Christ's baptism in the waters of the Jordan and the construction of the first baptisteries? What brought those very waters to such an extreme state of distillation? Aside from the aforementioned need on the part of the early Church to abolish pagan mysticism (especially that surrounding its last enclaves: the miraculous sources), there was an ever-growing tendency within society itself toward the occult. Profoundly affected, no doubt, by the barbaric invasions and the ensuing collapse of the Roman Empire, populations in the West, suffering from penury, recurrent terror, and dislocation, had begun looking for some eschatological response. From the immediate to the remote, the palpable to the impalpable, human sensibility underwent—at this very time—a profound transformation. So, indeed, did ritual. The suppression of river baptisms and their substitution by baptisms in consecrated basins reflects such a transformation.

Aside from the earliest baptisteries in the Near East, such as one at Dura-Europus (which was little more than an architectural accommodation to an existing structure), baptisteries proper began to be constructed in the fourth century according to a certain prescribed plan: as independent, freestanding edifices rising up from a square floor and capped by a high overriding dome or cupola. Reviewing a descriptive catalogue of over four hundred known baptisteries, one may readily note that this plan underwent innumerable variations and modifications, yet the archetypal model remained astonishingly constant throughout.[3] Over and over, the square of the floor plan, symbolic of earth, found itself—in elevation—transformed into the circle of the vaulted dome, symbolic of heaven. The one, however, only emerged into the other through the intermediary of yet a third geometric configuration: the octagonal. Indeed, no form would more fully characterize baptismal architecture than this eight-sided polygon. Whether described by the immersion bath itself, by a surrounding colonnade, or by the overall floor plan—its four corners bisected by an equal number of oblique wall panels or apsidal recesses—the octagon served as signature to the total construction. Semiotically charged, it represented—in the symbology of numbers—deliverance, emancipation. For the catechumen or initiate, about to enter into the folds of the Church by the ritual of immersion, it designated, in fact, nothing less than spiritual rebirth.[4] If the number seven signified the union of the body (four) and the spirit (three) as manifest, say, in the seven virtues or holy sacraments, eight—as delineated by the octagon—announced an entirely new existence. Based on the eighth day—the day that transcends the calendrical seven—it spelled for the catechumen the *dies natalis* of resurrection.

In Gruter's *Inscriptiones antiquae*, one finds a three-line poem by Saint Ambrose (339–397) touching upon that very ordinance:

> The baptistery, to merit its name, should be eight-sided;
>   Out of respect for that very number, faultlessly assembled;
> That there, where baptism occurs, the individual, in
>   reemerging, be reborn.[5]

One comes to realize that not only had the waters been channeled into a rigorously circumscribed milieu by the fourth century, but the milieu itself had become subject to a strict codification. In visiting, for instance, the baptistery of Riez in the Alpes-de-Haute-Provence (fig. 6), one is immediately struck by the cryptogrammic program inherent in such a structure. About a narrow eight-sided baptismal pool, eight granite columns stand as if in sentinel. This colonnade, in turn, creates a ringlike ambulatory about the surrounding walls of the edifice, which—themselves faceted into eight distinct recesses (alternately rectangular and semicircular)—create yet another resonant scale in this reverberant structure. Altogether, eight echoes eight on three distinct registers, generating a numerical harmony that seems to radiate well past the confines of the baptistery itself.

Figure 6. The Baptistery at Riez (Alpes-de-Haute-Provence). Courtesy of Musée Paul Arbaud (vi, VII, 19), Aix-en-Provence.

Built on the ruins of a Roman bath that had promoted, once, the health of the human body, the baptistery—in evangelizing that pagan site—came to celebrate the triumph of the spirit in its relationship, now, with a remote divinity. Withdrawing further and further from a world rife with disorder—its cities pillaged, its populations decimated, its countrysides set ablaze—the early Christian sought refuge in that very remoteness. Increasingly esoteric, sign came to replace effigy as a vector of access (see "*Terra Sigillata*" and "Venus Disfigured," pp. 29 and 44). Not only the architecture of baptisteries and their adjacent basilicas, but music, liturgy, and whatever little remained of the graphic arts (most especially, mosaic) underwent the selfsame codification. For the next five centuries, a reign of signs, symbols, numeric signifiers would replace the resemblant. Each, in its own redundant manner, would point in the promised direction of that celestial realm.

By the eighth century, the construction of baptisteries in medieval France would have ended altogether. "In a capitulary of 789, Charlemagne declared that, henceforth, not adults but only children in their first year were to be baptized. This act would put an end to the construction of edifices independent of the church for the sole purpose of baptism. . . . Such structures would now be replaced by baptismal fonts inside the church proper."[6]

From that first all-determinant baptism within the flowing waters of the Jordan to the delicate sprinkle by aspersion inside the basilica itself, this initiatory ceremony—seemingly immutable—would have been subject, in fact, to the irrepressible forces at play within the ever-evolving field of human ideation. For at least four centuries running, however, it would leave—like so many monumental imprints—these stout hieratic structures. Despite their dereliction, baptisteries such as that of Riez—kaleidoscopic in its radiant octagon—seem, today, to have arrested time itself. In that inexorable movement *away*, they mark a moment in the history of that very ideation in which faith, seemingly, crystallized. And, against its own growing remoteness, found haven—for those four centuries running—in number.

The Deletion of Shadow

The Sarcophagi of Arles, II

One can trace the stylistic evolution of sarcophagi throughout the diacritical fourth and fifth centuries in any number of ways. The materials employed, the ateliers involved, and—most especially—the subject matter treated, all serve as indices in elaborating the history of that development. It is a period, one discovers, fraught with change, transformation. In considering subject matter alone, one goes from the tumultuous figuration of bodies depicted in deep relief—characteristic of late Greco-Roman classicism—to an ever-increasing sobriety in which the human form serves no longer to decorate but, rather, to instruct. Released from the "antique mêlée," the figure propagates, now, as a pedagogical vector, the virtues of the new faith.[1] Doing so, it tends to grow detached from other figures, isolating itself upon the horizontal plane from all corporeal contact, while undergoing—in terms of perspective—a marked reduction in relief. As a plastic entity, the figure moves—slowly but ineluctably—toward its own effacement.

To appreciate this phenomenon fully, one needs to recall the theological imperatives at play at this time, and the aesthetic effects they had upon the sarcophagi themselves. Emerging out of the rich figurative representations of late antiquity that recalled the pleasures of life such as hunting, harvesting, or the erotic foreplay of libidinal forces thinly disguised as cavorting cupids, early Christian sarcophagi, to the contrary, tended to celebrate the promises of a life to come. "In opposition to the fleeting glimmer of life as expressed by Catullus's *breuis lux*, the *lux perpetua* of light eternal becomes, paradoxically enough, the aspect that is most real—most meaningful—in all human existence."[2]

At first, this profound transformation expressed itself with reticence, drawing on biblical scenes from the Old Testament that were essentially pastoral, even reminiscent, in nature. By the second half of the fourth century, however, the carved panels of sarcophagi had grown markedly rigid, architectonic, hierarchical. Within a brief period of time, they expressed themselves in terms no longer narrative but symbolic. They'd hardened into theophanic, eschatological scenographies that reflected the growing obsession with what lay beyond—within the invisible reaches, that is, of the everlasting. One need only read the following passage from Cosmas Indicopleustes to recognize the level of ideation early Christians had attained in contemplating the divine. Speaking of God as unique, without antecedent, Cosmas qualifies his presence in the following manner: "invisible, impalpable, incorruptible, immortal, impassive, incorporeal, unlimited, indistinguishable, and indivisible."[3] In a single word, God—and, by extension, the God-like—had become, in graphic terms, undepictable.

Little wonder, then, that in tracing the stylistic evolution of sarcophagi at this particular time, one has the distinct impression that the richly carved relief of their foreground is being steadily absorbed—as if assimilated—by their underlying background. That the "rampant play of volumes and their superposition on a number of distinct planes, suggesting as it does a tridimensional space that perfectly reflects sensorial reality," is being suppressed, now, in favor of a resolute abstraction.[4] Bit by bit, the body—one realizes—is being subsumed by the word; phenomena, by speculative vision.

As a measure of that gradual yet inexorable transfiguration, one might consider how the very signature of carved relief—to wit, the shadow itself—came to vanish. Deeply ensconced, at first, within the underlying folds of the marble panels, it enhanced the glistening soaplike luster of the raised foregrounds. It provided, as such, a chiaroscuro effect between the lit surfaces and their channeled interiors, creating thereby an impression of depth, dimension, that served—in terms of perspective—"to situate the individual within a universe of his or her own measure."[5]

Not only the full figures themselves and the deep, overlapping folds of their costumes, but—thanks to so much meticulously worked surface—the flare of nostrils, the corner of lips, the interstice between toes came to fill with that ephemeral substance. The techniques employed for creating such effects were several. Chisel work gave a certain "fabric" to features such as heads, palm fronds, and architectural decor, whereas drill work *(trépanation)* afforded a far more pronounced effect upon the given surface. If, for instance, a running drill was employed to create channels within a tuft of hair or the flowing mane of a lion, a single blow of that drill would delineate—say—a tear duct or dimple. In whichever case, the cavity was created for the selfsame purpose: as a receptacle for shadow. Functioning in counterpoint, the shadow flooded the voids, brought the entire panel into dramatic relief.

Gradually, though, these cavities and the dark, malleable properties they contained would vanish. Writes Georges Duby: "Under the influence of Plotinian philosophy and a spirituality that rejected the shadow as a manifestation of matter, depth was abolished, and—along with it—carved relief."[6] One can follow this attrition throughout the latter half of the fourth century by a chronological inspection of the sarcophagi. There is, at that time, a steady breakdown in perspective as foreground and background merge. Drill holes, for instance, grow shallower and shallower, and the impression of depth that they once provided progressively diminishes. The pupil of the eye, for instance, finely bored at an acute angle for the sake of enhancing relief, finds itself, henceforth, thinly incised at the center. The overall countenance, as a result, takes on a flat, depthless demeanor. Not only human figures but the decor that surrounds them undergoes a like impoverishment. Acanthus leaves, for example, no longer overlap but lie arranged on a single plane, at the expense of plasticity.[7] As perspective vanishes, so does detail. Increasingly devoid of identifying characteristics, figures tend to face outward, removed from the very world that once enveloped them. Disassociated, they harden into static, isomorphic, and—finally—lifeless representations.

One feels, in this steady effacement of the figurative, the beckoning of invisible forces. As the Empire itself suffered division under Honorius (395) and Rome fell to Alaric (410), with all the ensuing disorder that those events created, the promise of "a world to come" must have exercised an immense attraction on the beleaguered populations. That world, though, could only be conceived, addressed, approached, by the bias of the verb (see "Venus Disfigured," p. 44 above). Not until the advent of the Romanesque, a full six centuries later, would it once again be invested with a plastic terminology of its own: with, that is, a full set of figurative equivalents. Meanwhile, throughout the late fourth and early fifth centuries, the figure continues to lose depth, dimension, corporeality. More and more, it appears to float free of its underlying baseline, no longer subject, it would seem, to terrestrial gravity. In a late attempt to prevent all such representation from vanishing entirely, sculptors resorted to outlining a given form with bold undercut channels. This technique *(cernure)* provided a crude, even degenerate, sense of depth to a particular work: one acquired by a uniform incision of the panel itself rather than by the elaboration, on raised planes, of proper relief. It continued to be employed, however, until—finally—the figure vanished altogether in the latter half of the fifth century. With it, the shadow—indissociable from its instigating figure—vanished as well.

It would be tempting to compare the demise of figuration in the early medieval with that in our contemporary world: how, in each case, form found itself replaced by sign; a visual apprehension of existence, by an abstract conceptualization. Such a comparison, however, would be misguided. If our own cybernetic systems have done little but codify, and, in codifying, reduce the given world to an even more rigid set of human controls, early Christian theology proposed a world altogether different. It projected well past itself not a replica but the program for a redemptive, all-remedial existence, exempt of each and every mortal contingency. Product of an intense imaginary fervor, that world was populated by figures that—by their very dissimilitude—defied any form of graphic representation. Within that world, the entire dramatis personae of the blessed, resplendent with shadow, would find themselves absorbed—as if obliterated—within the uniform plane of the sarcophagal panel, and the panel, in turn, would be reduced to the pure silence of prayer, meditation, incommensurable faith.

City of God

for James Hajicek

One always arrives, it would seem, too late. Even here, alongside a winding mountain road, reading a monumental Latin inscription carved upon an overhanging rock ledge, one is left far more puzzled than properly enlightened. Dating from the first third of the fifth century, the inscription commemorates nothing less than the founding of Theopolis, the City of God. Fortified by ramparts and gateways *(muros et portas)*, according to this description, it would surely have left substantial proof of its existence. But where, exactly? Year after year, archeologists, historians, and the culturally curious such as myself comb these high, deserted plateaux in search of some small indication. For the City of God could not have vanished altogether. It would have left earthworks, crop marks, potsherds, even, say, a few meager bronze coins placed between the teeth of its defunct to serve as *viatica*. But no, next to nothing remains if not the "working hypotheses" of the specialists—conjectures that fill the silence of these otherwise mute, windblown expanses.

Figure 7. Monumental Latin inscription at Saint-Geniez-de-Dromon (Alpes-de-Haute-Provence). Photo by the author.

One might begin, nonetheless, with the inscription itself (fig. 7). It states, in nineteen lines of deeply incised Roman capitals, that a certain Claudius Postumus Dardanus, the retired praetorian prefect of all Gaul (a position that would rank him second only to the emperor in power), accompanied by his wife, the noble Nevia Galla, and his brother, the illustrious Claudius Lepidus, ex-consul of the German provinces, had broken through the flanks of a mountain to provide a viable access *(viarum usum)* to this very city. They'd done so, it's stated, for the general good: for everyone's security and well-being *(omnium voluerunt esse commune)*. In a place they'd chosen to call Theopolis *(loco cui nomen Theopoli)*, they elected residence.

What, though, would someone of such high rank as Dardanus, along with his immediate family and an entourage of an estimated five hundred souls, be doing at this altitude, confronting cold, extreme aridity, and a scarcely arable soil? Why should the highest-ranking members of a patrician class abandon all the splendor and privilege of Arles, the imperial city, and willingly submit themselves to such hardship?

There are two possible responses to this question: one, touching on the weltanschauung at that given moment in late antiquity; the other, on Dardanus's specific condition as both a public figure and a private individual. These two responses, however, overlap: one cannot entirely isolate one from the other. Leafing through the pages of any history book dealing with this pivotal moment in Western history, a reader can't fail to be struck by the profound transformations occurring at this time. On every conceivable level, the Western world—Rome, that is: bureaucratic, imperialistic, deeply reminiscent—is breaking down, falling apart; and another world—the early Christian: still tenuous, susceptible, drawing more on the promise of a distant felicity than the offer of some immediate gain—is beginning to assert itself. Increasingly, this alternative world has the favor of an exhausted, disillusioned populace. Even among the most privileged classes, it will attract those who have come to recognize the fragility of the established order, more and more subject to invasion from without and moral deterioration from within.

The newfound fervor will take many forms, not the least of which will be the quest of the "desert," of the *loci deserta*. Beginning in the Holy Land itself, there is a virtual flight from the cities, from the moral and spiritual decadence that those cities have come to represent, and a search among the fervent for "the invisible, the impalpable, the incorporeal, the immeasurable."[1] The distance *taken from* one world will come to equate itself with the *approach toward* another: that of imminent salvation. Ascetics of all orders will install themselves in grottoes, rock overhangs, whatever patch of forsaken ground promises—by its very poverty—access to the Kingdom of God. As one historian has put it: "By the start of the fifth century, this 'nostalgia for the desert' had become European."[2] Some of society's most eminent figures, according to Saint Ambrose, had begun retreating into the mountains. Dardanus would be no exception.

Added to this, Dardanus had his own personal reasons to retire from that crepuscular world of late antiquity, despite all the privileges that his high office afforded. He'd seen Rome fall to Alaric the Visigoth in 410, and Alaric's successor, Ataulphus, prepare to attack Gaul immediately after with an army of seventy thousand. By an astonishing act of diplomacy, Dardanus had managed to convince Ataulphus not only to spare the remainder of the Roman Empire but—wonder of wonders—restore the Empire to its original splendor. Ataulphus, moreover, had his own *raison sentimentale* for wishing to do so: he'd fallen in love with his prisoner, the notoriously beautiful Galla Placidia, who also happened to be the emperor Honorius's favorite sister.

This whole venture, however, was short-lived. Even if Ataulphus and Galla Placidia were married in Narbonne on the first of January 414 with great pomp and ceremony—a marriage that promised everlasting peace between their two belligerent peoples, Latin and Barbarian—within a year Ataulphus's alliance with Honorius had dissolved. In September 415, Ataulphus was assassinated, Galla Placidia tortured for her betrayal of her people, and Dardanus—dismayed by the fickleness of human emotions—driven to an irreversible decision: to retire from all human affairs and dedicate himself to the worship of God.

In making this decision, he was counseled by the greatest spiritual figure in all of Christianity: Saint Augustine of Hippo. Beyond the rich exchange of letters that they both enjoyed, it's likely—historians feel—that Saint Augustine enclosed, along with letter number 187, a copy of a freshly completed chapter from his great opus, *The City of God.* This letter, dating from the summer of 417, would have reached Dardanus only months before he and his entourage left Arles behind to head for their own City of God high in the Alpes-de-Haute-Provence. They'd have done so illuminated by the beauty and fervor of Saint Augustine's words: "Two loves have built two distinct cities. Love of self at the expense of God, the terrestrial city; love of God at the expense of self, the Celestial City. One basks in its own glory; the other, in that of the Lord."[3] Toward that *civitate Dei, in monte sancto ejus,* they'd make their way, casting aside all fortune, all privilege, all earthly amenity. Chanting, no doubt, as they went, singing vespers by torchlight and matins by the first rays of the morning sun, this community of early Christians—freshly converted for the most part—were moving, in Saint Augustine's words, "toward a sabbath that knows no night, a kingdom that knows no end."[4] By their very fervor, they marked as they went the end of antiquity and the outset of a faith that would serve, according to Saint Augustine, as a "novitiate for all eternity."

Here I am, then, fifteen centuries later, looking, as numerous others have done, for some slender trace, some irrefutable clue to that vanished city. How could the carved Latin inscription along the roadside that promised so much have yielded, in fact, so little?

Had the signifier, here, totally eclipsed the signified? Even worse, had it pointed, in its grandiloquent evocation of a fortified *locus*, to little more than some ephemeral cluster of dwellings? Some long-since dismantled assembly of drystone hovels? Dardanus, after all, was well into his sixties, perhaps even his early seventies, when he founded Theopolis. What if he'd had the inscription carved more as a declaration of intent than a description of fact? Given his great age, he might never have had the time to erect that massive stronghold dedicated, as it was, to the contemplation of God.

There have been, however, just enough chance discoveries, both within the earth itself and in the subterranean depths of archival deposits, to warrant curiosity and an ongoing search for the City of God. Speculation has essentially concentrated on two specific areas lying on either side of a small Alpine *commune*, Saint-Geniez, fifteen kilometers east of Sisteron. Saint-Geniez alone, by its very toponym, invites speculation, for Saint Genès was a third-century Christian martyr and the object of a fervent cult in the city of Arles, where he is still celebrated as a patron saint. Had Dardanus, in abandoning Arles for his mountain retreat two centuries later, brought a femur, a knuckle, a collarbone of this venerated figure along with him? Nothing would have been more characteristic of his times than the transfer (the *translatio*) of such a worshipful object (see "Relics," p. 35 above). Indeed, whole communities would come to prosper about a few coveted ounces of osseous material enshrined in bejeweled reliquary boxes and housed in subterranean crypts. If, however, Dardanus actually had brought a bit of Saint Genès's mortal remains along with him, only the place-name today (despite its slightly different spelling)—on road signs, letterheads, the town hall—still testifies to the fact.

Just west of Saint-Geniez and within two kilometers of the inscription, one comes to the first of those two proposed sites for Theopolis. Lying in a vast natural amphitheater, a *cirque* of several thousand square meters bound by a ribbon of rock cliffs, above, and a mountain stream, just below, the site attracts by its boundless pastoral splendor. *Vastus,* I hear myself thinking; the word in Latin doesn't mean immense but void, empty, desertic. *Vastae solitudines,* Geofroy le Gros would intone in the eleventh century, *quasi altera Ægyptus:* an Egypt of one's own, that desert which, upon entering, Saint Jerome would equate to a second baptism. In sites such as these, the ascetic would be not only fleeing the spiritual blight of the cities but approaching—by the bias of that very void—"the place wherein every charisma and theophany," as Jacques Le Goff has written, "becomes possible."[5] For under the immense unbroken dome of the desert sky—that of the Holy Land—hadn't monotheism first emerged? Authors as diverse as Ernest Renan in the nineteenth century and George Steiner and Vincent Scully in the twentieth have made the exact same observation. Polytheism thrived in a sharply delineated landscape of hills and valleys (e.g., Greece and Italy), whereas monotheism always depended on the presence of an unbroken, uninterrupted—one might even say cyclopean—heaven directly overhead. *Vastus,* indeed.

And as I make my way uphill along a narrow drystone sheep run, I can easily imagine Dardanus and his entourage settling under this blue dome. For Saint Paul of Thebes, the desert consisted of "a mountain, a cave, a palm tree and a spring."[6] Here, of course, there are no palm trees, but a mountain that in no way obscures the immensities overhead; caves for immediate occupancy; and an abundant spring within easy reach. The *vastus* here—the void, that is—could only invite, in such circumstances: plenitude itself.

Material evidence, however, remains sparse. Bits of Gallo-Roman storage jars *(dolia)* and roof tiles *(tegulae)* have occasionally been unearthed after a deep winter's plowing, as has a single Gallo-Roman tomb. A peasant, in digging a deep grave for his dead horse in the 1920s, came across the remainders of the grave site. But a single tomb doesn't make a city any more than a swallow makes a spring. Furthermore, this form of burial—the body housed in *tegulae*—was practiced over several centuries and cannot be dated with any accuracy. All that remains, then, as material evidence, are a few sections of broken wall in the nearby hamlet of Chardavon. These sections, exceptionally thick, were probably part of a small monastery founded in the eleventh century that— according to the Cartulary of Saint Victor, dated 1035—belonged to the Order of Saint Augustine. Had this early Romanesque brotherhood come to commemorate, six centuries after the fact, the memory of that first Christian community, inspired by Saint Augustine himself? Had it built its walls out of the collapsed masonry of that lost Theopolis? Nothing is less certain. For even if the hamlet is located at the base of that *cirque*—that broad, gently sloping pastureland—and nearly five kilometers closer to the inscription than the second proposed site, it would be hard if not impossible to encircle that open, exposed area with fortifications, with those ramparts and portals that Dardanus had erected for the security of all: *constitutum tuetioni omnium.*

The second proposed site, the Oppidum of Dromon, located two and a half kilometers east of Saint-Geniez, gives greater promise. There, nestled among jutting Alpine boulders at an

altitude of twelve hundred meters, one finds all the natural pre-
requisites for a mountain stronghold. "Dardanus had been a general as well as a prefect," one historian reminds us, "and knew full
well that by connecting those towerlike boulders with high defensive walls, he'd be creating a fortress, a *castrum*."[7] Within, a small
protected area—nine thousand square meters—could thus be
circumscribed. Today, in wandering about that tiny mountain
promontory, even in the absence of any fortifications, one feels
closer to Theopolis than ever before. Directly beyond—immense,
weightless, irreal—lie the Alps themselves, capped in *neige éternelle*,
while below, far below, a valley resonates with the slip of an inexhaustible mountain torrent. Isn't this one of those privileged places
in which "every charisma and theophany" might have once been
possible? For here, at this elevated remove, one directly confronts
those *vastae solitudines*. Here, one can easily imagine those early
converts entering at last into that ardent, long-sought communion.

What's more, within this natural platform, a somewhat anonymous rural chapel, reconstructed in the seventeenth century, hides
in its substructure a crypt of great historical significance. Even if
specialists have differed widely as to the date of its construction
(Henri-Irénée Marrou attributes it to the Byzantine or fifth century; Fernand Benoît to the eighth or ninth; Jean Barruol to the
tenth or eleventh), one is in the presence, here, of an exceptionally
archaic structure. Curiously enough, the same specialists who
differ in regard to its dating all agree on its original function. It
served as a *martyrium*: a place in which some venerated figure had
been interred. Which figure, though, one finds oneself asking?
Was it Saint Genès d'Arles, whose relics Dardanus himself might
have deposited in the fifth century? Or the reputed remains of

that very saint transferred, at a later date, by the Benedictines of Saint-Victor, Marseille? For at Dromon, the latter had established an important priory of their own in 1030. Such a priory would require, for the sake of its resplendence, the magnetizing presence of sacred bone. Only such bone could draw pilgrims from considerable distances and endow even the smallest ecclesiastic complex with a lustrous aura of its own.

One might even speculate on the possibility that Dardanus and his wife, Nevia Galla, had been buried or reburied, sometime later, within the crypt. In studying the medieval, one can only be struck by a continuous practice of commemoration: a site, for instance, in which a hermit or thaumaturge might have dwelled in the fifth century will be commemorated in the eleventh by the construction of a chapel, church, or monastery. The *lieu*, centuries later, will find itself reconsecrated and the memory of some blessed figure, ceremoniously reinstated. "Wouldn't the remains of Dardanus and Nevia Galla have been enough," Benoît asks, "to suscitate a cult of relics for these remote Alpine populations?"[8] Wouldn't they, indeed, one can only answer.

Furthermore, a nineteenth-century historian, the Abbé André, accumulated a certain amount of verbal evidence in regard to a "pillar" discovered by a shepherd in 1763 among the rubble of the collapsed chapel of Dromon.[9] This "pillar" was clearly a *cippus*, or a low, commemorative column; such columns had served in late pagan antiquity and early Christianity as altarpieces. This particular *cippus*, however, possessed two distinguishing characteristics. First, it was inscribed in Greek. Even if the *cippus* with its inscription has long been lost, it has left historians puzzled. Had Dardanus himself been Greek, as many have speculated? His name alone raises the possibility, not to mention the distinctly

Greek toponym he'd chosen for his mountain retreat: Theopolis. The second distinguishing characteristic bears upon a square alcove or recess within the column itself. The shepherd, Honoré Masse, described this alcove as something that had been firmly sealed with a ceramic tile. Driven by curiosity, no doubt, he'd broken this ceramic seal and was astonished to discover "une odeur suave"—a sweet scent—issuing from within. Even if Honoré Masse never elaborated on the contents of this alcove—on the origin of that delectable fragrance—one can be fairly certain that he'd just uncovered, quite unwittingly, human relics. According to specialists, a *cippus* could have contained little else.

Relics, but whose? One comes closer and closer, it seems, to so much increasingly evasive evidence. Even here, at Saint-Geniez-de-Dromon, surrounded in the aura of that lost city, there still isn't a single shred of substantiating proof that one is actually standing on that sacred ground. As for myself, I need to ask what, in fact, had I been looking for? Was it the city itself? The lost location of that altogether eloquent locative? Or perhaps it was some trace of its auroral promise, here in a late world where such fervor, such an unlimited investment in the powers of the redemptive, has all but vanished. Readers of residue, of vaporous matter, we always arrive, indeed, too late. Here, in this extended aftermath, I've come to wonder, as pseudohistorian, whether history itself—that vast, self-obliterating compilation—isn't little more, finally, than a delectable scent, *une odeur suave*. Whether, in fact, one might not be satisfied with such a haphazard collection of whiffs, rumors, lingering insinuations. For Theopolis, at least, it might very well be the case.

Laying the Dragon Low

Once, there were dragons. No more than three hundred meters from my home, a Romanesque chapel commemorates the site on which one of those winged reptiles—the hard product of a collective hallucination—had been brought to bay by its captor: a young proselytizing miracle worker, Saint Véran. By a simple sign of the cross, Saint Véran managed to subdue and enchain the enormous creature, reducing it—by his very gesture—to a state of piety. For years, the dragon had been ravaging the countryside, slaughtering humans and devouring flocks, leaving in its wake a thoroughly traumatized population. The mere sight of this monster had stricken that population with terror. According to one historical source, its impenetrable scales glowed with a ghastly pallor, and its smoldering breath belched forth in pestilent flame (*flammam horribilem evomebat*).[1]

Today, it's easy enough, of course, to interpret this hallucinatory phenomenon, issuing as it did at the outset of the sixth century, from a late pagan, profoundly rural society (even the Latin word

ST·VERAND·P·P·NOUS ⟸ A· CAVAILLON CHEZ·

Figure 8.   Saint Véran and the dragon. Woodcut from the Bibliothèque municipale d'Avignon, *Estampes*, Atlas 8, no. 218. Photo by Esther Sobin.

for pagan, *paganus*, implies rurality, rusticity). Fraught by successive invasions, by all the destruction and ensuing famine caused by marauding parties of Ostrogoths, Visigoths, Franks, and Burgundians, these very last pagan populations came to polarize their anguish, clearly enough, upon the figure of the dragon itself. "Famine alone," Aline Rousselle writes in her provocative *Croire et guérir,* "can create psychic disorders, among them the illusion of being devoured alive."[2] Saint Véran's dragon, in all probability, was nothing more than such an illusion. It was called a *coulobre* in contemporary legend, a Provençal word meaning either snake or dragon. Semantically, there's nothing to distinguish one from the other. What might have been, in fact, but an immense grass snake (the *couleuvre de Montpellier* can attain, in these regions, a length of four meters), this common reptile could easily have found itself magnified into a creature of mythical proportions. Famine alone might well have driven these distraught populations to hyperbolic extremes.

By investing the snake with all the characteristics of the dragon, they could, in turn, accuse that legendary creature for the misfortunes that had befallen them. Thus designated, it gave the local population a small if consequent measure of psychic control over the anguish they must have suffered in confronting so many successive waves of barbaric invasion. Now, at least, a surrogate cause could be attributed to all that devastation. Proximate, even familiar in its legendary nature, the dragon as devastating agent could be located *within* their immediate environment rather than feared as an interloper from without.

What's more, it would serve Saint Véran perfectly in his evangelizing mission. For it gave him the ideal opportunity to prove to the local populace the superiority of the new faith. Still languishing in the superstitions and folklore of late paganism, the people needed to be awestruck by a yet higher order of magic. Saint Véran only had to admonish the dragon in the name of that order, summon it to kneel, and draw before its eyes the sign of the cross, thereby bringing the creature to bay, to exhibit his immense, thaumaturgic powers. The enthralled public, in way of response, hastened to convert. Clearly Saint Véran represented in their eyes, now, the agent of salvation itself. The dragon disarmed, demystified, leashed to the saint's wrist, must have appeared, at last, in its true nature: that of a hapless reptile. Days later, it could be released into the surrounding countryside that he and he alone could claim to have pacified.

The legend of Saint Véran and the dragon is traditional enough. It borders, in fact, on hagiographic cliché. It contains nothing that doesn't strictly conform to the life of other early miracle workers in Gaul, from Saint Martin of Tours onward. All the elements are present: an evangelizing saint as hero, his or her encounter with a mythological creature embodying the evils of an obdurate paganism, and the saint's ensuing triumph over that creature in the name of the new faith. This traditional legend, however, might well conceal another. Like a stratigraphic deposit, it might easily overlie an even deeper level, immediately beneath. Without in any way dismissing the foregoing account based on early Christian lore, one might consider, at least, an older, more arcane level of interpretation. One might even ask whether one dragon, here, isn't dissimulating another.

Saint Véran had quite deliberately elected to live at the Fontaine-de-Vaucluse. It was there, in fact, that he first encountered that winged reptile. In the early years of the sixth century, the Fontaine represented one of the last bastions of pagan mysticism in southern Gaul. Located at the source of the River Sorgue, its waters were considered miraculous, and the cult of those waters drew pilgrims, suffering from a variety of illnesses, from considerable distances. Indeed, sites such as these, profoundly rural and reputed for their curative powers, were the very last to undergo Christianization. Pilgrims, upon arriving, would pitch offerings into the source itself: votive money, metallic plaques, carved inscriptions, effigies of the affected organs for which they sought some form of relief, if not outright restoration. In every respect, the magic of such sites lay inscribed within the collective consciousness. Despite a series of anathemae pronounced by the Church vigorously banning such cults, these sites continued to curry the favor of the poor, the ailing, the destitute (see "The Blossoming of Numbers," p. 52 above). Even bathing in such waters at the time of the summer solstice, "be it at night or in the early hours of day," would be forbidden by Caesarius, bishop of Arles, as late as 542.[3] Such practices, however, were deeply rooted. They dated from pre-Roman, even—perhaps—pre-Celtic times. Water cults were profoundly autochthonous in nature. Even an early Christian apologist such as Marcellus would be drawn to such remedial methods. "When you see the first swallow," he wrote in 395, "fall silent and run to a fountain or source and bathe your eyes therein and pray to God that your eyes won't suffer, that year, from the swallows' perniciousness."[4]

How, then, could these waters be demystified—"demagnetized"—in the name of an alleged greater mystery? A greater "magnetization"? Quite clearly, they had to be divested of their magic—their curative magic—in the light of so much firmly held popular belief. The waters, in short, had to be neutralized. According to the early Christian Father Tertullian, didn't the devil himself love to linger in water? "Immundi spiritus aquis incubant," he'd write.[5] Among demons, he'd proclaim, there was a predilection for springs, fountains, sources. Which demons, though, one might ask, if not the *draci immanissimi* themselves: those monstrous dragons that speckle the pages of Judeo-Christian mythology. Poisoned by Daniel, slain by Saint George, crushed underfoot by the Emperor Constance II, these ultimate enemies of the human race—whose decomposing bodies alone could pollute the surrounding air—had to be eliminated at all costs. For it was the dragons, as the *genii loci* of the sources (among other attributes), that perpetuated the water's mystery. By eliminating the dragons, one could—by that very act—banalize the mystery itself.

How, though, could this pernicious reptile, the vile serpent of Eden, the very embodiment of evil, have ever been considered a guardian spirit, the friend of Aesculapius and the gentle companion of the Lares, those household deities? Throughout classical mythology, this fire-breathing monster was endowed—quite manifestly—with *a second set of characteristics*. It not only repelled, it protected. Pliny speaks of such a dragon within the walls of Tiryns that defended the city's inhabitants but destroyed with its poisons any invader.[6] As the fierce guardian of the golden apples of the Hesperides as well as the golden fleece of Colchis, the dragon was fraught—one discovers—with duality, ambivalence. It's an ambivalence, however, that the new faith could scarcely tolerate. Rather than associating, it tended to separate one inherent characteristic from another, isolating, dichotomizing, establishing as it went a vertical division between the world of the winged, the fleet-footed above, and that of the scaly, the ground-hugging below. The former would rise now in blessedness, whereas the latter—subtle, surreptitious, unpredictable—would be relegated to the lowest ranks of existence.

Leo et draco est: leo propter impetum; draco propter insidias.

Both the lion and dragon exist, Saint Augustine would write: speed being the characteristic of the former, treachery that of the latter.[7] In only a matter of a few centuries, dragons such as the *sacri dracontes*—the venerated guardians of the Bona Dea in Rome—would have fallen into profound disrepute. Christianity had recast this mythical creature in an entirely new role. Deprived of its ambivalent nature, it had become—for that early medieval world—the emblem of evil incarnate.

One may safely assume that at the Fontaine-de-Vaucluse the dragon's traditional role as guardian of the source had undergone a similar devaluation. The protector had turned monster; the custodian of the waters, cannibal. Clearly, a struggle of monumental proportions was being waged by this nascent mysticism in its attempt to establish—in place of so many deeply rooted, ancestral earth cults—the uniform vision of an all-buoyant, all-redemptive heaven. The metaphysical had come to replace the physical; the impalpable, the immediate; the veneration of an invisible deity, that of the resurgent waters.

Even more, though, than banalizing the mystery inherent within those waters, the nascent faith would attempt to neutralize, now, the evanescent spirits that dwelled at their depths: the very nymphs, that is. There is archeological evidence that a *nymphaeum*—a temple dedicated to those creatures, consisting of a central basin surrounded by a colonnade and sculptures depicting them in all their gracility—existed at the Fontaine-de-Vaucluse. This would have been typical, of course, of any water sanctuary in Gallo-Roman times. It would be Saint Véran's mission, in fact, to desacralize if not demolish this temple and build alongside it an oratory in honor of the Virgin Mary.[8] Fountains, springs, the points at which hidden water sources suddenly erupted, were associated—since prehistoric times—with the female, the *Mater Magna*, the telluric entrails of the earth mother herself. It's not for nothing that Saint Véran would seek to replace one form of goddess worship—that of the nymphs—with another—that of the Virgin Mary. He well realized that this transmission could only occur if that exclusively female attribution were respected in an uninterrupted manner.

Today, one can safely speculate that the much-maligned dragon—accused of having devastated the land and decimated the population—had protected not only the water sanctuaries throughout antiquity but the nymphs themselves. One can even assign a benevolent role to the guardian of those "life-giving goddesses," as Aeschylus called them. Without the dragon's protective cover, these water spirits—richly endowed with a variety of therapeutic virtues and commonly known as the *nymphis medicis, nymphis salutaribus, nymphis salutiferii*—would have been routed from their subterranean haunts and rendered powerless, inoperative. The dragon tamed, the waters neutralized, the resident nymphs disseminated, these late pagan populations could do little more than yield to the evidence. Saint Véran, quite clearly, was propagating a far more effective magic. Collective conversions immediately followed, and one of the very last thermal sanctuaries in southern Gaul underwent, in the name of the new faith, deconsecration.

A full eight centuries later, the Fontaine-de-Vaucluse's most illustrious resident, Francesco Petrarca, would evoke those nymphs in his *Vita Solitaria:*[9]

According to Seneca, the sudden welling up of a source deserves altars. What source, indeed, is worthier than this one? Furthermore, I've sworn to Christ that I'll erect such an altar . . . close to the fountain itself, no, not to the nymphs nor the local divinities, as Seneca would have it, but to the Virgin Mary, whose fertile virginity and ineffable maternity overturned all the altars and reduced each and every temple to rubble.

One can only speculate on the immense cost of such a profound psychic displacement. The elaboration the new faith—contingent as it was upon the promise of an afterlife—could only occur at the expense of a deep-seated devotion to the proximate, the sensorial, the tellurically invested. A heaven aglow with the new word had come to replace the inveterate magnetism of an earth, generator of its own rich therapeutic properties. The dragon, in this sense, had been one of earth's most steadfast guardians, the staunch sentinel at every one of its miraculous springs. It had kept watch over the reclusive, the indigenous, the nymphs in their deep underwater retreats. So doing, it had preserved the idea of a world redolent with its own inherent mysteries. Uprooted, rarefied, those very mysteries, henceforth, would rise. The atmospheric would replace the chthonic; the divine word, the animated object. Buoyed by a host of new signifiers, Mary would ascend, now, into an inaccessible *elsewhere* from which dragons, nymphs, and all the attendant representations of the telluric would be not only excluded but relegated to the lowest possible realms of existence. At its own risk and peril, a new age—the *Christiana tempora*—had come to replace them.

~~~

The Dark Ages

A History of Omissions

A particular period in history is remembered, principally, by the vestige it leaves: those material deposits wherein it might, unmistakably, be recognized. From the end of the sixth century to the outset of the eleventh, however, Provençal history can be characterized by a dearth of vestige, not to mention an extreme paucity of recorded documentation. It's a history that can be written—according to one of its finest specialists—in little more than a few pages. "Following a period of marked conservatism, a slow erosion gradually accelerates in an irreversible manner toward paroxysm. Historians can only begin to measure the extreme violence of that epoch by the virtual absence of testifying source materials."[1]

The rare documentation that survives is notoriously self-reflective. It only records what falls within the narrow spectrum of individual or collegiate concerns and self-interests. It gives no idea whatsoever of collective realities. Church records, for instance—such as cartularies, in which charters and title deeds to estates are compiled, or capitularies, in which ecclesiastical

ordinances are recorded—don't in any way reflect prevailing circumstances. Indeed, they do little more than confirm episcopal
privileges and prerogatives. Their silences, however, might be
more eloquent than their terse, cursive testimonials, which themselves tend to fade, in turn, within a brief period of time. "For the
historian, everything grows obscure toward the end of the sixth
century. At a moment when the life of cities had fallen more and
more into the hands of bishops and their episcopate structures,
the interruption in church registers can be read as an indication
of the disorder and disorganization that prevailed at that time."[2]

Private source materials such as correspondence, chronicles,
journey books, and wills, reflecting for the most part personal
concerns, shed hardly any light upon a world that continues to
narrow, dim, asphyxiate. In the wake of Roman civilization and its
monumental collective realizations, the *regnum francorum* in
Provence from 536 onward does little—it would seem—but degenerate. Not only is the nascent Merovingian kingdom divided
against itself, but a succession of external events—some discrete,
some simultaneous—come to diminish the little that remains of
socioeconomic coherence within the beleaguered region. Plague,
for one, will decimate entire populations. From the end of the sixth
to the middle of the eighth century, five successive waves of that
deadly epidemic will send city dwellers scurrying into the countryside, depopulating urban complexes such as Arles and Marseille.
Indeed, the desertion of cities for one cause or another—be it
partial or complete—will characterize the early medieval until the
beginning of the eleventh century.

Invasions, of course, constitute yet another factor. If Provence
had already suffered the incursion of barbaric tribes from the second half of the third century onward, several of which—

Burgundians, Ostrogoths, and, finally, Franks—came to settle and establish themselves as so-called barbaric successor states, other ethnic societies—Lombards and, somewhat later, Saracens— would pillage and lay waste large portions of the territory. The Saracens were particularly active along the Mediterranean, attacking the ports of Marseille, Arles, Narbonne, and Agde repeatedly from the first third of the eighth to the last third of the tenth century. These attacks would undermine, even further, the last abiding networks of exchange, especially that all-critical trade route between the Mediterranean and the newly established urban centers to the north: to wit, the Rhône Valley.

If plague, barbaric invasion, and the internecine struggles that arose within the emergent kingdom might be considered the principal causes for that collective breakdown that we've come to call the Dark Ages, one might consider, even if briefly, its disastrous effects. Chronologically, the first of those effects entailed a dramatic falloff in population. Already apparent in the latter days of the Roman Empire (Emperor Majorian, in an attempt to promote repopulation, forbade girls to take the veil before the age of fourteen and ordered widows to remarry within five years), the demographic decline took on startling proportions from the fifth century onward. Agrarian societies, subject as they were to recurrent invasions, had to contend, as a result, with a breakdown in trade, communication, and reciprocal exchange. Isolated, they began living off whatever little they could cultivate, entering— inexorably—into a subsistence economy of endemic scarcity. One can safely assume that such circumstances brought about a concomitant decline in sanitation, with minimal medical care— conditions that could only provoke a substantial decline in the birthrate. It was scarcely an epoch, furthermore, that encouraged

natality. "The falloff in population created a falloff in food production," writes Renée Doehaerd. "This, in turn, reduced the
population even further, reinforcing, thereby, the very causes of
penury." It was a vicious circle that would characterize the life of
Western societies for the next four centuries. "A poor harvest no
longer implied what it once did. Now it designated a society that
fed on weeds, clods of earth, on rotting cattle and human flesh.
Now it designated death, depopulation." Radulfus Glaber bore
witness to a world in which "famine had reached such proportions
that grown-up children ate their mothers, and mothers, their
babies." Such an extreme state of deprivation induced hallucina-
tions, as well. The author of the *Annales* of Moselle recounts how,
in the spring of 793, people thought that they saw wheat growing
in abundant quantities in fields, forests, marshlands. "They could
see it, they could even touch it," he relates, "but they could in no
way eat it."[3]

Just as historians are struck by the inertia of those populations, by their inability to respond—over so many successive
centuries—to such dire circumstances, archeologists are astonished by the virtual absence of typologically distinct, chronologically evolving, artifact. Extenuated, deprived of both the means
and materials of production, the Provençaux could do little more
than recycle what they already had. They produced nearly nothing
of their own. The region itself was in no way affected, furthermore, by the "invigorating forces of renewal inherent in the
Columban movement" in the seventh century, and hardly
reacted—come the ninth—to the Carolingian dynamic of reform,
reorganization, and expansion.[4] It simply went on stagnating,
caught in the "torpor of those who know little more than the
rhythm of the seasons, than the brief span of their own lifetimes,

than the hours spent praying and intoning psalms, and the recurrent pangs of recurrent fear."[5]

If, as suggested, a period in history is remembered by the vestige it leaves, what—indeed—have those four centuries left posterity? In answer to that question, Dominique Carru, a prominent Provençal field archeologist, replied quite succinctly: "little more than bones and ceramics."[6] In regard to bones, they reveal—upon osteopathic examination—exactly what one would expect: an alarmingly high rate of perinatal mortality, and, for those who survived infancy, a life expectancy that hardly exceeded that of thirty years. Malnutrition, of course, accounts for the better part of those deaths, infantile or not.

As for the ceramics, one is left with plates and utensils that—over that extensive period—show no sign whatsoever of development, whether in their form or facture. Like those they served, they remain resolutely static. Gray, nondescript, devoid of all decor, this reduced-fired ware has been found fortuitously by archeologists digging for Gallo-Roman vestige on stratigraphic layers lying *immediately over*, or by those exploring Romanesque subsoils in areas *immediately beneath*. Either way, it represents for archeologists material belonging to a desolate interlude—an empty passageway—between two culminant moments in human history. Medievalists who specialize in that particular period, however, have no way of determining the date of that gray, nondescript ceramic unless it is unearthed in stratigraphic association with imports. For it's only the imports, in this instance, that serve as chronological markers. Without them, all sense of sequential order vanishes. Between the seventh century, when Asian and African ceramics suddenly disappear (due, no doubt, to the Arab invasion of Tunisia), and the beginning of the eleventh, when

Italian "forum ware" makes its appearance, there is simply nothing to mark time in the midst of so much dull, indeterminate autochthonous material.[7]

Other basic artisanal products fare far worse. Hardly any glassware can be ascribed to this period (for a rare exception, see the following essay), and ironware is virtually nonexistent. In excavating an eighth-century cemetery at Entraigues in the Vaucluse, archeologists found—by way of grave goods, or *viatica*—nothing more than a single rusted nail, in the midst of a graveyard that contained over fifty individual sepulchers. The rarity of such an artifact speaks for itself. As for buildings and building material, one is confronted with much the same poverty. Virtually nothing remains of the provisional dwellings that these sparse populations constructed for themselves. "The stone they no longer knew how to extract, transport, and carve vanished altogether and found itself replaced by wood as the primary building material."[8] Wood, daubed walls, and thatched roofs became the invariable components of structures that, long since vanished, have left nothing as vestige but the ghostly outline of their post holes. As sockets for anchoring wooden uprights, these post holes can be recognized, today, by the "differences between the colour and texture of their fill and those of the earth into which they were dug."[9]

If, by the latter half of the ninth century, large areas of France (especially in the north) had begun benefiting from an enlightenment that prefigured the Romanesque, Provence continued to languish in a profound state of torpidity. Subject to the violent conflicts that existed between Burgundian and Carolingian power interests, and gutted of most—if not all—of its natural resources, Provence could do little more than subsist at a material level, often compared to that of the protohistoric. Until the turn of the millennium, its populations would continue to live in small, autarkic communities at the very edge of the *agri deserti*, repeatedly subject to famine and drought, to clouds of locusts and showers of hailstones, not to mention the last—but still lethal—waves of Saracen invasion. If, by miracle, its long vanished wooden churches left, as vestige, a few scattered chancel barriers carved in local limestone (see "Celestial Paradigms," p. 107 below), little, otherwise, would remain to testify for four consecutive centuries of unremitting human misery.

Historians, by the nature of their discipline, are given to collect, classify, and correlate their amassed materials in a coherent, sequential order. "One can scarcely be surprised, then," writes one specialist in regard to that age, "by the malaise historians feel in confronting so much indeterminate matter."[10] For Provence had fallen into the shadow of an all-obliterating eclipse. Now neither vestige nor documentation would come to testify, and—in testifying—clarify layer upon layer of resolute obscurity.

It's just there, perhaps, where history escapes historians, that the greatest dangers might be said to lie: there, in default of all testimony, at the heart of mnemonic obliteration, that history is most liable to repeat itself. For that reason alone, the Dark Ages deserve all the consideration—all the painstaking examination—that they might possibly receive.

The Blue Tears of Sainte-Marthe

per far veyre

Situated at the base of a cliff, Sainte-Marthe is the place-name, the *lieu-dit*, of an area terraced in orchards, vineyards, and, occasionally, long rectangles of ground gone fallow. On one such rectangle, on a dry summer day, one can find by simply scuffing the earth with the edge of a sandal any number of blue, tear-shaped beads. They're drops, droplets, really: the debris of a small early-medieval glassworks. I'd come upon this area, as one comes upon most things, quite by accident. It covers no more than thirty or forty square meters of uncultivated soil, and constitutes, I'd learn, a characteristic part of any historic glassworks: that area in which waste was disposed of.[1]

Despite its profound state of dereliction, the site, I came to discover, is immensely evocative. One can easily enough imagine those drops—those blue tears—dripping, centuries earlier, off the white-hot nozzles of blowing irons. As a poet, glass—I must admit—has always fascinated me. Indeed, I find the process of glassblowing remarkably similar to that of composing poetry, for

in each, one brings totally disparate substances together, be they
the sand and flux of the parison or the scattered instances of the
poem. Then, by an abrupt increase in temperature—be it caloric
or intellectual—those substances are brought to fusion, inseparability. They undergo a transformation, moving from their original
opaque state to one of pure transparency: from darkness to light.
Moreover, in both glassmaking and poetry, the human breath—
inextricably involved—finds itself enveloped, englobed, in the act
of its own elaboration.

Among the droplets, I'd also managed to find a few splintered
bits of finished glass. From these I could safely assume that the
glassworks were early medieval, belonging to that span of indeterminate history we so aptly call the Dark Ages. More, though,
than the facture of the splintered bits themselves, thin as broken
eggshell, it was their color—that pale, translucent blue—that
helped indicate the period of their fabrication.[2] Unmistakably,
they belonged to the late seventh or early eighth century: the last
moment before glassworks vanished altogether from Provence
for a full four hundred years.

Then, too, the fact that such a *verrerie* was located at the base
of a cliff was, I'd discover, perfectly characteristic of those times.
A cliff provided four advantages. First and foremost, its flanks
must have abounded in holm oak and aleppo pine: with the indispensable firewood, that is, for the ovens. Concurrently, it kept
the glassmakers from encroaching on cultivated or cultivatable
ground. Thirdly, the cut wood could be slid down the slope
rather than dragged up from under. And lastly, cliffs offered
readymade abutting walls for provisional shelter. For glassworks
of this sort were temporary affairs. They lasted exactly as long as
did the surrounding firewood (or, inversely, as long as the terms

of a contract, allowing for the exploitation of such a wood, stipu-lated). The workers, upon arrival, would construct little lean-to hovels for themselves, employing drystone for the walls and long branches bound in puddled clay for the roofs.

And Sainte-Marthe? How long had it survived as a glassworks? Judging by the extent of the waste deposits that I'd come upon, no more, perhaps, than two, three years. My assumption here, needless to say, is nothing more than that: a calculated guess in the face of so much obscurity.

Aside from wood fuel for the ovens and the abundantly available clay for the crucibles, silica—accounting for at least sixty percent of the glass's composition—must have come from the sandbanks of a nearby river, the Coulon. On the other hand, flux—the alka-line base that turns glass into a vitreous paste and allows for its malleability—must have been imported from a considerable dis-tance. A swamp plant called marsh samphire or saltwort or—by extension—glasswort was being cultivated, one may safely assume, within the Rhône estuary. A halophyte growing in saltwater marshes, the plant is rich in sodium. Flowering in winter and ripening in summer, marsh samphire, once harvested, was left to ferment—somewhat like lavender—in tall stacks. At the given moment, it was distilled in small underground kilns lined at the base in clay and covered at the top by a whole network—a mesh, really—of turtle shells. Just enough space was left between these shells to serve as flues, points from which the accumulated vapor might dissipate. Once cooled, the ash of this plant—carefully screened—was processed into hard white balls, fit for transporta-tion. From the Rhône estuary to Sainte-Marthe, it would travel a distance, I calculated, of no less than a hundred kilometers: in those troubled times, a remarkable achievement.

And so, I came to discover, water was part of the process. For the sodium contained in that plant is essentially marine. Add to this earth in the form of silicates, fire in the white heat of the ovens, and air, of course—blown in sharp blasts down the full length of the blowing irons—and one has the four elements reunited. Reunited, that is, for the sake of crafting the most ephemeral, perhaps, of all human products: glassware.

None of my own reading or rudimentary field research, however, helped me to understand who, exactly, they were, these itinerant glassmakers. Nor what kind of life they really led, moving from site to site, hovel to hovel, exhausting the surrounding wood fuel as they went, and leaving little more than these droplets—these transparent blue tears—as mementos. For scarcely anything else remains today. I'd searched for an oven—for traces of some provisional, makeshift furnace. During the early medieval, these rustic structures comprised little more than two rows of massive stone laid upright over bedrock, then capped with flat overlapping slabs. The ensemble was then caked in layer after layer of refractory clay. Inside, the walls of the kiln widened somewhat into a womblike chamber, while remaining open at either end like a wind tunnel: open to the north (the wind-dominant side) for generating fire, and to the south for creating draft and removing ash. Hard as I looked, though, not a single trace of an oven at Sainte-Marthe could be found.

Curiously enough, it's the dead, lying in their sepulchers in medieval necropolises, who've helped conserve the rare pieces of intact glassware we possess from this period. Discovered occasionally, in archeological soundings, with a goblet to the right of their face and tilted in the direction of their mouth or, in the case of ecclesiastics, held flush against their chest, they've lain there—the guardians of that fragile ware—gradually decomposing as the glass itself, bit by bit, has gone iridescent. Aside from the dead, however, and random scraps of notarial documentation, we know almost nothing. True, there are a few Romanesque frescoes in the area belonging to a far more evolved period, centuries later, that depict glassware in scenes such as those of the Last Supper. But of them, of those, of the glassblowers that moved—itinerant— through the Dark Ages of so-called historical time, even the specialists can do little more than speculate.

One is left, in fact, with a period of time—over four hundred years—that has gone, for the most part, unrecorded (see the previous essay). There was, perhaps, far too little to record. This is true in terms of not only its glassware but nearly every other manifestation of human activity. Living as I do in the heart of Provence, I find myself continuously confronted with this apparent lacuna in history: this lapsus in its unraveling. In examining architectural vestige, what's more, one could easily extend that sterile expanse of four hundred years to a full thousand. Aside from a little humpback stone bridge, the Pont-Julien, built in the time of Augustus, there is architecturally no standing structure within the immediate area between this stalwart conveyance, built in 23 b.c., and the first smattering of Romanesque chapels that date from the outset of the eleventh century. Everything else either has been razed by successive invasions or, constructed out of wood, has long since decomposed.

One wonders, living in a time such as ours, whether a similar period couldn't recur. Whether, indeed, in its own surreptitious way, it hasn't already begun. Of course, our own Dark Age, were it to develop, would be luminous: luminous with neon, cathode ray, with the green screens of countless monitors functioning autonomously in some postlinguistic semiotics, determining every aspect of our lives, shaping not only our decisions but our very choices. Yes, a dark, an incandescent dark, that would have no further need of those very creatures—ourselves—who'd first wired its circuits and set its screens aglow. Haven't we already entered that age, that shadow, the edge of that terrestrial eclipse? Aren't there signs sufficient enough: not the least of them, the steady, ineluctable breakdown in literacy as we move, today, from the verbal to the visual. From an articulated culture to one electronically programmed. From a consciousness rooted in speech to one in which so many neurons react spontaneously to so much optical stimuli. To life, in short, as video game.

As if foreshadowing that age, there are movements today (growing in both number and influence) that would break language down into strict literal units. That would make of literality a *diktat*, preparing us, thereby, for that ultimate codification. Post-Marxist, postmodernist, posthumanist, they'd gladly ban, if they could, metaphor from accepted usage. "Blue tears," for instance, is metaphor. It's drawn, like all figures of speech, from a free play of the imagination, and motivated by the need to weave—reconcile—the disparate parts of one's experience into a common fabric: a fabric by which societies, throughout history, have come to recognize themselves. By association, resemblance, correspondence in the Baudelairean sense of the word, metaphor has always allowed us to create—against irrefutable, totalitarian fact—the common chords of what was once called a common culture.

Tears, blue tears. They'd left us that much, hadn't they? They who'd blown—out of molten parisons—those globes, those viscous bubbles no thicker than their breath, had left us, in the midst of so much apparent debris, eloquent testimony.

As for ourselves, as we gain control or—what amounts to exactly the same thing—*lose* control over our own ecosystem, it's hard to think that the future won't depend on how we read—examine—vestige such as this. Won't depend, for instance, on how we come to interpret four hundred years of virtual silence that left us—at Sainte-Marthe, at least—with little or nothing if not its tears. Its blue tears. The long pendulous waste of its blue translucent tears.

❧

The Blind Arcade

Reflections on a Carolingian Sarcophagus

> In offering up flesh and figure to the essence of withdrawal,
> that very invisibility takes possession of all worldly visibilities.
>
> Marie-José Mondzain

Occasionally, a nondescript work of little apparent interest, either aesthetically or historically, can take on unexpected significance when considered in context: relative, that is, to the unraveling of the full cultural fabric. Such is the case with a roughly executed Provençal sarcophagus dating, most likely, from the tenth century. Indeed, its carved decor—a frail, unconvincing set of archways bereft of all human figuration—speaks not only for its own moment in time but for its place within the running continuum. For this "Sarcophagus with the Arcade Decor" (fig. 9), as it's called—a limestone parallelepiped 1.8 meters long, 63 centimeters wide, and 53 centimeters tall—perpetuates in its own barbaric manner a motif that originated with the Gallo-Roman over a thousand years earlier. From the outset, this motif, architectonic in nature, consisted of a series of alcoves or compartments, each of which was vaulted by an archway overhead and bracketed by columns on either side. These compartments might be viewed as discrete stages within an overall scenography wherein an individual or group of individuals would establish their identity—their very role—in relation to the visual drama depicted on either side. The stages themselves, invariably odd in number (usually five or seven), thus allowed for a central stage in which a predominant figure stood portrayed. In pagan sarcophagi, this figure might have been that of a god or goddess, or an effigy of the defunct therein entombed. In the transitional period that followed, marked iconographically by an early Christian assimilation of pagan motifs, this central figure was often that (among others) of the Good Shepherd: Christ, that is, in pastoral disguise (see "Crypto-Christianity," p. 20 above). Then, in the overtly Christian period that ensued from the mid-fourth century onward, it increasingly became that of Christ Triumphant or his heraldic counterpart: the Christogram. Throughout all three periods, this central figure serves—both visually and thematically—as the vertical axis for these predominantly horizontal compositions. Neither axis, however, comes to dominate the other in frontal panels that celebrate—be they pagan or Christian—some particular aspect of the everlasting.

Before examining the sarcophagus in question, it is useful to consider how the figures housed within these arcades developed over the three given periods, in terms of both their execution and their rapport with the surrounding architectural environment. For the "Sarcophagus with the Arcade Decor," bereft of any figuration whatsoever, marks the demise of that very motif, its point of total attenuation. Such a degree of graphic degeneration, however, was long in evolving. One might even say, in retrospect,

Figure 9. "Sarcophagus with Arcade Decor," monastery of Ganagobie (Alpes-de-Haute-Provence). Photo courtesy of Francois-Xavier Émery.

that that degeneration lay inscribed from the start. For the arcade decor predicated a separation—a segregation—of graphically clustered figures into discrete units: the aforementioned compartments, or auxiliary stages. So doing, it broke up the sensuous conflation of antique figures, represented—more often than not—as anatomically inseparable. Often erotic, even bacchanalian, these sepulchral panels that once celebrated life in the most jubilant manner underwent a deliberate set of constrictions. Isolated one from the next, the actors in these antique mise-en-scènes found themselves relegated to disparate, if parallel, roles. Their dramatic significance within the energetic field of the fusional mass was therefore critically reduced. As a result, the central figure (often emblematic of the emperor himself) came to dominate the entire panel all the more preponderantly. In such works, one can readily detect the emergent influence of Neoplatonism. From the late third century onwards, it propagated a philosophy of renouncement, detachment, and sublimation that would scarcely encourage graphic work celebrating the free play of libidinal forces. Quite to the contrary, it tended to mystify existence. It represented its privileged cast of characters in an increasingly remote, hierarchical manner. Ensconced within the central archway, these figures, in turn, came to dominate—one might even say, monopolize—one carved panel after another. If this schematization is scarcely evident in sarcophagi dating from late Roman antiquity—wherein the figures, though isolated by the intervening columns, remain remarkably distinct, readily identifiable, and, above all, equal to one another in both stature and significance—it will, by contrast, totally determine the configuration of Christian bas-reliefs by the end of the fourth century. Not only do the figures grow increasingly isolated and relegated in size according to rank, but they assume a stiff, remote, lifeless appearance. Individuated portraiture had become, by then, generic, stereotypic. Furthermore, figures that had once been carved in deep relief scarcely rise, now, over the underlying surface. By the beginning of the fifth century, foreground and background planes tend to merge, coincide, and the figures themselves appear to lose all substantiality (see "The Deletion of Shadow," p. 59 above).

Before the figures vanish altogether, one finds them framed within blind arcades that have grown increasingly factitious. As renderings of architectural ensembles, the arcades possess less and less structural validity. They're far more the memory of a viable ensemble than an accurate depiction. Frequently, one finds oneself gazing, in fact, at little more than so much schematic decor. There is no attempt, henceforth, at verisimilitude, in either the treatment of the arcade itself or the emblematic characters that stand as if stultified between each of its columns. One is witness, at this time, to the invasion of the sign at the expense of all graphic representation. Simultaneously, the rendering of depth—of figuration in the third dimension—undergoes suppression. Within that diminishing perspective, symbol will come to supplant image: the anagogically implied, the graphically invoked. "The funerary art of those three centuries [the third to the sixth] leads in a myriad of ways past all earthly contingency, by a simplification of form to that—ultimately—of message."[1] One finds oneself gazing, indeed, at a vision of an exhausted world, a world that has abandoned all hope in any form of earthly felicity for that, finally, of a distant, eschatological promise.

"You heard a voice speaking but saw no figure; there was only a voice," one reads in Deuteronomy 4:12. In this critical moment of semiotic transformation, that figure, in fact, will vanish altogether. In the absence, henceforth, of any form of human representation, geometric patterns, insignias, and obsessively repeated motifs will invade the iconographic field with ever-growing insistence. Gregory of Nyssa (335–394) would compare the image to a book, a conveyor of language. What can't be seen can—at least—be said: carved, that is, in so many stylized cryptograms across the lids and panels of these funerary vessels. From the beginning of the sixth century, one enters into a world of symbolic codifications so perfectly repetitive that it becomes virtually impossible for art historians, today, to determine the date of a particular work with any accuracy. Until that time, the fabrication of a given sarcophagus could be estimated within, say, an interval of twenty, thirty years. Now one is suddenly confronted with an expanse of time devoid of any evolving characteristics whatsoever: a time in which civilization seems as if locked in stasis. "From the tombs of late antiquity to those of the year 1000," writes a Provençal medievalist, "we are left completely in the dark. This is true not only for the body's last resting place but for human habitat as well."[2]

Where societies had continuously marked their passage by a slow but irrepressible series of inventions, deletions, all-but-imperceptible modifications in the crafting of artifact—detectable today in whatever vestige happens to survive—the Dark Ages left, for imprint, little more than an arrested signature.

Only against such a backdrop can the sarcophagus in question be properly considered. Here, too, however, it seems virtually impossible to determine its date of fabrication with any assured accuracy. Estimates have varied from the mid-Merovingian (seventh century) to the more probable late Carolingian (tenth century). Whichever it be, this work clearly belongs to that indeterminate, indeterminable period in human history in which history itself—as seen, at least, in retrospect—appears to have stopped.

In examining, for instance, the execution of its arcade, one immediately remarks that no attempt whatsoever has been made to describe a given architectural reality. More than sham, the decor has become perfectly abstract, illusory. The image, it might be said, has turned to outline, and outline, to a barbarous form of shorthand. As for human figuration, it, too, of course, has long since vanished. Gone, now, the saints, the miraculously resuscitated, the apostles strolling beneath palm fronds. Gone, too, the perfect sets of archways that served, once, to aureole those figures—no matter how indirectly—in so many overriding half-circles. Instead, a work such as the "Sarcophagus with the Arcade Decor" represents a world bereft of all earthly determinants. Rather than represent, it relegates. "Relation by its very essence," Thomas Aquinas would declare, "is not something in itself but *tends* toward something."[3] Invisible, impalpable, that "something" could only be conveyed by the graphic description of voids, lacunae: by the desolate celebration of a profound metaphysical omission.

It should be noted, moreover, that this work belongs to a period in which construction had virtually ceased. Aside from drystone hovels for provisional shelter during periods of invasion and structures—mostly ecclesiastical and military—in wood, building, from the seventh century onward, had come to a halt. This very sarcophagus reflects such a state. The loss in one medium— architecture—is all too apparent in that of another: bas-relief. This is particularly true in regard to the manner in which the arcade itself has been rendered. For a people who had lost the art of constructing vaulted arches—keying stone to stone in overhead assemblages—could scarcely be expected to carve such a structure in relief with any verisimilitude. Indeed, the rendering here is perfectly factitious. No arch resembles another in either design or dimension. As for the columns, they're far too svelte, and the capitals, far too ungainly, to support such an overriding mass. Degenerate, the entire arcade rests upon a stylobate, a flat pediment, that appears to float entirely free of any underlying foundation. In fact, the whole arcade appears to float—fictive, irreal—as if suspended in a hallucinatory architecture of its own.

In addition to this illusory quality, the number of arches in its arcade happens to be even: thus, the possibility of a center— of a central compartment in which a human figure might be portrayed—can only be excluded. There is neither a natural point of focus in a lateral reading of the work nor a perceptible depth in a frontal one. One's attention, in fact, alights nowhere. There's no place any longer in which it might.

As a late lingering trace of classical antiquity, the blind arcade decor will vanish altogether from Dark Age sarcophagi. The Age, in fact, had become that of the aniconic: of a silence so profound that not even the slightest geometric device—the least barbaric embellishment—would diminish an aphasia that had grown, by then, replete. Aside from a few scattered chancel barriers (see the following essay), the absence of graphic signature testifies for a period in human history in which a profound division had fallen between the perceived and the professed; between, that is, the nominally visible and the divinely envisioned. The Age, indeed, had turned into a tyranny of dissimilitudes. Until the advent of the Romanesque, nothing further could be *said* because nothing, any longer, had been *left to say*. If the "flesh" of antiquity had been converted into the "word" of early Christianity, that very "word," now, had been rendered—for the duration, at least, of that dark interlude—mute, unutterable, forbidden.

Celestial Paradigms

Nothing remains of the ephemeral wood-framed Carolingian churches in Provence if not, occasionally, an ornamental stone screen. These chancel barriers, as they're traditionally called, once served to separate the choir from the nave immediately beneath, and constituted, in that "civilization of wood," the only durable structural element in the entire edifice.[1] Outlasting their original function, these chancel barriers can only be found—in Provence, at least—out of all architectural context. Reemployed on the walls, buttresses, crypts, and belfries of Romanesque churches, or—at an even greater remove—displayed in museums or on public monuments, they no longer serve as anything more than ornamental panels (fig. 10). In terms of function, they've gone from the liturgical to the decorative.

They deserve, however, particular attention, as they testify to a moment in cultural history that's almost totally devoid of artifact (see "The Dark Ages," p. 85 above). Any indication that might be gleaned from these displaced works, issuing as they did

Figure 10.   Inextricable symmetries: a chancel barrier reemployed within
the lower crypt of the Cathedral of Sainte-Anne, Apt (Vaucluse). Photo by
P. Foliot and G. Réveillac, courtesy CNRS, Centre Camille Jullian, Aix-en-
Provence.

out of the depths of a profound silence, can only be considered invaluable. More, though, than the panels themselves (usually of modest dimensions), it's the motifs with which they've been carved in shallow relief that endow them with a profound historical and spiritual significance. Invariably geometric and symbolic, deliberately redundant, they depict tresses, tendrils, spirals, and foliated scrolls that, in twining, envelop one another in inextricable patterns that know—it would seem—neither beginning nor end.

This geometric interlace pattern, as it's called, emerged out of northern Italy somewhere toward the middle of the seventh century and made its way across all of Gaul. Its origins, though, remain obscure. Some specialists consider that a bitumen slab, engraved with a cruciform interlace motif and dating from the Susianian (circa 3000 B.C.), constitutes its first appearance. Others reach back even earlier and attribute its origin to a coiled serpent ornament prevalent in archaic Mesopotamian art. Whatever its origin, however, one can be perfectly certain that the pattern arose out of the Near East, and moved—inexorably—westward. And, as it did, two factors came into play. Concurrent with its loops, braids, and tresses, it introduced into the Western world a highly stylized graphic vocabulary that would replace—within a relatively short period of time—Greco-Roman figuration (see *"Terra Sigillata,"* p. 29 above, for an equivalent transformation). More, though, than merely disseminating that eminently symbolic vocabulary, loosely enveloped in the folds of its indolent ellipses, it came to weave the daisies, helices, double palmettes of that oriental idiom into an intricate mesh of its own making. It not only enveloped: it embroidered. Indissociable from those motifs, it would serve to determine their tenor, elasticity, and interrelatedness in an increasingly codified manner.

Transiting, no doubt, through Greece, the geometric interlace pattern served Roman iconography, at first, only as peripheral decor. By the latter half of the third century, however, it had begun spreading its formal diagrammatical patterns over entire surfaces. In place, say, of some pastoral vista depicting nymphs and a cohort of bacchanals in close pursuit, a field of six-pointed stars—meticulously interlaced—comes to invade the full mosaic. In fact, in studying the evolution of the interlace pattern, one grows to realize how it serves as an index of sorts to the sociopolitical, cultural, and spiritual climate at each given historical moment. As the Empire dissolves, for instance, the pattern tends to tighten. As it falls, subsequently, into the hands of barbaric successors, the very same loops, braids, and tresses not only tighten, they come to lock—clamp shut—about their own decorous armatures. By then, early Christian societies in the West, subject to recurrent invasion and extreme penury, had entered into a perfectly abstract appreciation of existence. Rather than celebrating life on earth in all its sensorial plenitude, they'd begun elaborating celestial paradigms that bespoke the eschatological promises of an all-redemptive afterlife. Eliminating not only the human figure but any reference, henceforth, to earthly existence, they created a scenography that depended on nothing but the hypnotic beauty of so much monotonous pattern: what, ultimately, would "occupy the conscious mind with some demanding but repetitive task (such as a mantra or rosary)."[2]

By way of example, one might compare the foliage scroll prevalent in late antiquity—resolutely open, rampant, describing its own meanders at will—with the closed interlace pattern that ensued. If the former might be characterized by the free circulation of its constituent elements, wherein both beginning and end are perfectly detectable, the latter, "enclosed on all sides by its lines, leaves no place whatsoever for any additional decor, no matter how minor."[3] From the open to the closed, the flowing to the fixed, one has entered into a realm of immutable realities. The interlace pattern neither invites nor repels: it subjugates. Caught in the stellar configurations of its richly interwoven tresses, the devout could do little—one imagines—but yield to its monodic splendor.

It's this very pattern that would enter Gaul in the mid-seventh century and come to constitute the standard decor of Carolingian chancel barriers in the two centuries that followed. It gave expression to a universe closed, as if hermetically sealed, on all but the sacred. In default of a viable alternative on earth, it proposed—in its inextricable symmetries—a schematic glimpse of the paradisical. There was, indeed, little else to anticipate throughout that arduous period but the *extra mundum fieri:* a world well beyond that of all human vicissitude.

If, as suggested, the interlace pattern might be read as an index of sorts to the conditions that prevailed throughout that entire period, one might consider—by way of conclusion—its propensity not only to enclose and self-envelop but to withhold. For in the tuft of its rich interwoven tresses, it acted as repository wherein the spiritual energies of entire populations—by the bias of sign— found expression. When, however, that obfuscated age drew to a close, those energies—long circumscribed—sought release. The tresses in which they once found themselves confined—taut, retentive, inviolable—could, at last, come unbound. Could pour, abundantly, forth. Emblematic of the forces at play at the outset of the Romanesque, that released field could be deployed, now, in the figuration of angels and apostles, of fantail mermaids and star-studded magi. The constraints of one age would provide, ulti-mately, for the dynamic of the next, but only after those *saeculae obscurae* had come—mercifully—to a close.

Vaulting the Nave

> The vault in its contours, borne by the solidity of its underlying walls, brings the entire structure to completion just as the flower—in drawing from the stalk—will convey to the tip of the pistil the very sap of its roots.
>
> Raymond Oursel

Nothing more fully marks the arrival of the Romanesque in southeastern France than the construction of stone churches, in particular their crowning achievement: the vaulted nave. At that auroral moment in Western civilization, the resuscitation of the vault might well be considered—in architectural terms—its "principal innovation."[1] Such construction, however, was slow in coming, characterized, at first, by trial and error. For springing a vault required not merely a knowledge of basic masonry—keying stone to stone against the framed truss of a temporary scaffold—but the ability to determine the stress that that overlying vault would exert on its supporting walls directly beneath, which was a far more complex question. That stress had to be received, contained, and absorbed, in default of which the entire structure could all too readily collapse. One may assume that before undertaking a given construction, the earliest Romanesque builders had an intuitive—if not a formal—sense of the equation that had to be met between the force exerted by the vault and the walls' powers to absorb such pressure.

Who were these builders, one might ask? Long before the edification of major basilicas—the work, quite clearly, of highly qualified architects—the earliest vaulted structures, modest in their ambition, bear the mark of itinerant masons. Lombards, for the most part, arriving from northern Italy in small artisanal *confréries*, these master stone carvers, often illiterate but bearing at the tip of their fingers all the genius of inherited traditions, studded the landscapes of Provence and Languedoc with the very first stout, austere, fully vaulted ecclesiastical structures. These earliest works, characterized by the "simplicity of their floor plans and the massiveness of their volumes," bore, as well, the unmistakable signature of their makers: the pilaster strip, or *bande lombarde*.[2] Essentially functional, these shallow projecting bands of masonry, set vertically in blind arcades about the exterior walls of early Romanesque churches, served as bonding agents against the instability of so much rubblework support. They thereby helped consolidate that support, "reducing cracking in the plaster and preventing longitudinal spread."[3]

One might mention, in passing, that before these deft, innovative craftsmen managed to vault an entire building, they erected a number of churches and rural chapels in their own inimitable style but covered with open timberwork roofs. Saint-Martin de Volonne, in the Alpes-de-Haute-Provence, is a case in point. Despite the length of this basilical edifice (twenty-three meters) and the fact that its five-bay nave was flanked on either side by aisles separated by "great round-headed diaphragm arches, resting on rubblework piers," its exterior walls were far too narrow (eighty centimeters) to support a fully vaulted overhead ceiling.[4]

This might have been the case for yet another edifice, the Priory of Ambialet in the Albigeois. Originally covered in timber, it underwent massive reconsolidation in the early twelfth century. The bays on either side of the nave were reinforced by barrel-vaulted arcades, and the arcades themselves by salient pilasters. At the same time, buttresses were placed flush against the existent pillars along the church's outer facades. These ameliorations—detectable today in a patient reading of the structure's rubblework masonry, devoid of its original plaster facing—endowed the edifice with enough stability to receive a full barrel-vaulted stone ceiling.

The "principal innovation," indeed. For now, one church after another could benefit from the invention—or, rather, the reinvention—of such an architectural structure, remarkable for both its solidity and its homogeneity. Infinitely complex in its manifold parts, work of this order—assembled according to a rigorous application of harmonic number—radiated simplicity. Upon entering an early Romanesque church such as Escales in the Aude, Saussines in the Hérault, or Lasplanques in the Ariège, one feels immediately enveloped by the inherent unity of so much low-hovering mass. Their walls are far too thick to allow for any but the narrowest of openings, and their capitals and cornice work far too elemental—inaugural—to allow for any but the simplest of decors. In structures such as these, one's attention is drawn—irresistibly—*inward*. One feels in such works that they were de-signed to contain—even withhold—the very mysteries they'd been called upon to commemorate. Vaults, arches, pilasters, and

Figure 11.   The chapel of Saint-Pierre de Montmajour (1030–1050), near Arles (Bouches-du-Rhône). Photo by the author.

bays, by their interrelatedness, collaborate in a singular attempt to embody—rather than merely diffuse—those mysteries.

Now the barrel-vaulted edifice could send the halo of its half-circle down the full length of the nave, endowing the entire work with the architectonic sign of the covenant. For here, in semiotic terms, the floor of the earth would have come to coalesce—at last—with the vault of heaven. Form, so doing, would have assumed the volume, contour, proportion, of faith itself. Furthermore, congregations could bask, henceforth, in the resonance of their own voices. Unlike the open timberwork ceiling that tended to absorb and thus neutralize liturgical chanting, the stone vault served as a kind of sonorous mirror. There, within those earliest Romanesque churches, the devout could not only proffer their devotion, but stand—as if enveloped—within the reverberatory shower of their own intonations. Thanks to the play of its masoned surfaces, the church had become, by the eleventh century, an acoustic chamber of remarkable quality.

The construction of such churches, however, called out, at first, for continuous modification. Only at the end of innumerable readjustments, by a process of trial and error, would the fully vaulted medieval edifice be brought to completion. In examining, say, the stout, austere, eminently spiritual basilica of Saint-Donat de Montfort (Alpes-de-Haute-Provence), one is immediately struck by the massiveness of its eight cylindrical piers in relation to the relative narrowness of its nave and side aisles, and the altogether hesitant treatment of its overhead vault. The line running down the summit of this vault tends to waver: rarely, if ever, does it manage to remain centered upon itself. Like the entire structure, it's caught—seemingly—in a series of equivocal gestures. It should be noted, too, that the vault of Saint-Donat isn't accompanied by the stabilizing presence of arch bands, which soon would rib virtually every Romanesque edifice, absorbing much of the pressure that such roofing exerted.

Yet another example of equivocation on the part of those earliest Romanesque masons is provided by the church of Quarante in the Hérault. No fewer than three distinct forms of arches are employed in its transept alone: "barrel-vaults in the north arm, groined vaults in the first bay of the south arm, oval cupolas on squinches above the transept crossing and the second bay of the south arm."[5] Clearly, one is witness throughout the first half of the eleventh century to an architecture in search of itself. Its power and originality, however, might well reside in the innocence of those auroral gestures: in the construction of so many massive, rudimentary, probatory works. For each, in its own manner, celebrates inception.

By the second half of the eleventh century, the discovery of the pointed barrel-vault would bring early Romanesque religious architecture to its highest level of accomplishment. Consisting of two equidistant curves that join at the vault's apex, the pointed barrel-vault relieved considerable weight from the overhanging structure, allowing—at the same time—the underlying walls to narrow in breadth and the windows encased in those walls to widen. One basilica after another, now, as if blossomed: blossomed with light, with a rich decor—be it painted or sculpted—that bathed in that light, and with a sense of buoyancy in their execution that allowed them to float free of that ponderous quality so characteristic of the earliest Romanesque. The work of highly accomplished architects—as opposed to immigrant, autodidactic stonemasons—it brought forth the very masterpieces by which Romanesque architecture came to be universally recognized.

Ever lighter, grander, and more luminous, the Romanesque would soon give way (in northern France, especially) to the Gothic, wherein walls, under an umbrella of slender, resilient, riblike members, grew virtually skeletal, reinforced as they were by spacious arcades from within, flying buttresses from without. Despite all the architectural mastery inherent in such structures, a critical element in their elaboration, however, found itself sacrificed. One after another, these consummate works, whether late Romanesque or early Gothic, tended—in their newfound verticality—to point, rather than inscribe; to release rather than enclose. So doing, they came to indicate a mystery that had grown—in the interim— increasingly remote and abstract, undergoing as it had a profound semiotic codification. Now that mystery could only be suggested—as if insinuated—by the dynamic thrust of so many masterful columns, spires, and pointed vaults, each of which gesticulated heavenward. Only in its absence—it would seem—could the godhead now be celebrated.

One returns, today, to any one of those relatively primitive early Romanesque churches and chapels—rural for the most part and often abandoned—with added respect, if not, indeed, marked reverence. Within their stout, barrel-vaulted frameworks, they managed, for the first half of the eleventh century, to confound signifier with signified, thereby incorporating the suppliant and the object of supplication within the low overhanging vault of so much rudimentary masonry. Together, one and the other as if coalesced, conflated, entered into a dialectic of pure reciprocity. Within chambers such as these, uterine in their all-inclusiveness, faith—it might be said—not only radiated, it massively resided.

The Dome

Architecture as Antecedent

He spredeth out the heauen like a vowte.
Esdras 16:59

If the fully vaulted nave might well be considered the principal innovation of early Romanesque architecture in southeastern France, the dome or cupola might be seen as its ultimate achievement. Coming as it did, grosso modo, half a century later (toward the end of the eleventh or beginning of the twelfth century), it capped one basilica after another in a simulacrum of the celestial vault. In the transfigurative spirit of the age, the dome managed to echo, even replicate—by the bias of metaphor—those otherwise inaccessible reaches. In bringing the eyes to rise, it raised the spirit. So doing, it offered the devout—by the articulated play of its volumes—a foretaste of those redemptive spaces in which all wrong would be righted; all obscurity, blissfully illuminated.

One of the finest examples of such a domed structure can be found at Saint-Martin-de-Londres in the Hérault (fig. 12).[1] Viewed from the exterior, the cupola is encased within an octagonal drum that emerges out of an exceptionally elegant basilical structure. Entirely outfitted in bonded small-course masonry, the basilica bears the unmistakable signature of its Lombard makers: the svelte pilaster strip. Once within this essentially trifoliated edifice (the nave was elongated in the latter part of the nineteenth century, disrupting its inherent harmony), one is drawn—as if magnetically—toward the transept crossing, not for the sake of the transept itself but for the dome that appears to float in an aureole of sunlight a full fifteen meters overhead. How the square of the floor plan manages to rise into the near circle of the cupola without the aid of either squinches (underlying supports) or pendentives (concave triangular sections for the underpinning of such structures) attests to the mastery of medieval stonemasonry. It does so, one learns, "by means of courses ingeniously hewn and corbeled out" so that the transition occurs in tiny, virtually imperceptible, increments.[2]

Throughout Western civilization, the square assimilated by the circle has always provoked wonder, amazement. In graphic terms, it might well illustrate our own most deep-seated aspirations: there, where the rational gives way to the spiritual; the predetermined to the incommensurate. In gazing at the cupola of Saint-Martin-de-Londres—floating, it would seem, like a virtually autonomous, self-sustaining unit high overhead—one feels a certain buoyancy and elation oneself. Indeed, in bringing the eyes to rise, it raises the spirit.

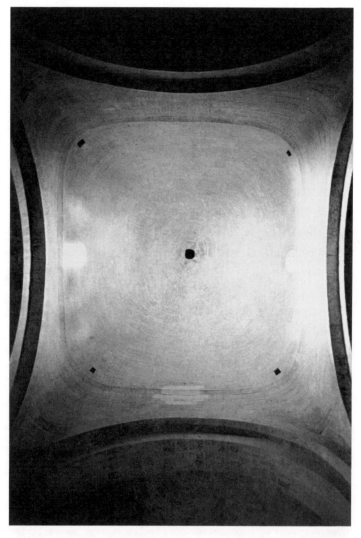

Figure 12.   The cupola of Saint-Martin-de-Londres (Hérault). Photo by
the author.

Such evocations of the celestial were long in evolving. Henri Focillon, in his *Art d'Occident*, suggests:

> We are most likely in the presence of one of those Oriental determinants that so profoundly affected the genesis of Christian art in the Middle Ages: what becomes evident, today, in examining the liturgy, iconography, and architecture of those times. The generalization of the cupola . . . over the transept crossing and the use of stone vaulting from the first half of the eleventh century onward constitutes—in fact—no more than a chapter in the history of those exchanges that began toward the end of the Roman Empire, declined throughout the early Middle Ages, and then reasserted themselves at the start of the Romanesque.[3]

Yet another art historian, André Grabar, in discussing the origins of Christian architecture in Asia Minor, examines one of the earliest instances of such a domed structure: that of Edessa in northern Mesopotamia. There, toward 525, in that flourishing period that extended from Constantine's conversion to the Arab conquest, a cathedral—considered one of the wonders of the world throughout Christendom—underwent construction. Long since vanished, it's only known to us today thanks to a long eulogistic poem written in Syriac by an eye-witness to its edification. Of all its many attributes, none receives more attention, therein, than the dome itself. "Sky of skies," the poet exults. "Its roof is spread open like the heavens, fully vaulted, self-contained," without the aid, that is, of any underlying columns.[4] One may assume from this description that the immense dome of Edessa, rising in a masterful play of corbeled masonry, must have rested on squinches, for without underlying columns and an adjacent ambulatory passageway, nothing else at that time in history could have supported such an all-imposing superstructure.

The squinches, four in number, would have represented the four corners of the world: the fixed points from which to admire— high overhead—that celestial replica in all its rotundity. The *éclat* of such a structure, furthermore, could only have been enhanced by the presence of so much scintillating mosaic. Against a field of glittering gold tesserae, it was the firmament itself in all its splendor that appeared to lie before the eyes of the dazzled spectator. Heaven's very mysteries stood, therein, as if depicted. "The microcosm of the Church," as André Grabar suggests, had come to replicate "the macrocosm of the universe."[5]

In earlier times, such domed structures—be they pagan mausolea or Christian martyries—had belonged to a strictly funerary milieu. Serving as tombs, they designated death, bereavement, and—by their overhanging cupolas—the conch of some purported assumption. Never before, though, had a "cube surmounted by a vaulted sphere" indicated a place of worship wherein the Eucharist might be celebrated.[6] Never before, that is, had such a domed edifice come to assemble the living in that most symbiotic of all services: Holy Communion.

It was out of such a context that Christian basilical architecture arose. Given a cruciform floor plan and a dome that seemingly floats over its transept, an architectural prototype could, at last, be established. It would take, however, a full six centuries for that prototype to reach the western Mediterranean from its point of origin in Asia Minor. Following a movement both monumentally slow and spiritually—ideationally—irrepressible, confronting on its way each and every obstacle that that darkest of ages presented, it would flourish by the outset of the twelfth century in a rich semiology of its own. As spectacular as it was reverential, the church found itself transformed into a theater of the sacred, celebrating—by the very play of its volumes—the promissory world that awaited the devout. By its architectonic program, it prefigured—in short—the redemptive.

Gazing up into the simulated heavens that the dome of Saint-Martin-de-Londres proposes, one can only be struck by the evocative power of such metaphor. As if weightless and self-sustaining, the dome has preserved, through the centuries, the splendor of its own hallucinatory device. It has done so, one might say, like a breath held—but tenuously—against its own impending exhalation.

Classical Roots,
Evangelical Branches

Antique ruins, lying for centuries in the fallow, windblasted landscapes of southeastern France, became—by the early twelfth century—sumptuous object lessons for architects bent on resuscitating classical traditions. Roman arenas, theaters, temples, and aqueducts—often in a pitiful state of dilapidation—underwent meticulous examination on the part of those architects. The ruins served as a kind of academy, according to one art historian, diffusing—*a silencio*—the otherwise lost doctrines of monumental construction. "Provençal Romanesque didn't so much submit to the influence of antique art as deliberately, methodically, explore each and every element it might possibly adopt for the sake of its own development."[1]

One can readily imagine that first generation of classicizing Provençal master builders. Instruments in hand, they must have gone about measuring, say, a massive barrel vault at the Temple of Diana in Nîmes or studying the exact manner in which finely hewn blocks of *lapides quadratae* were laid across given sections of an aqueduct such as that at the Pont du Gard. One can readily imagine, too, their fascination. For they were resuscitating, in that moment of reemergent humanism, not only the mechanics of classical architecture, but—inherent in its columns, entablatures, arcades—the very numbers of a long lost harmonic. Indeed, for well over six centuries, the laws underlying that harmonic had gone unheeded and ignored, and were finally forgotten. Now, though, in applying so much mute evidence to specific structural problems, the architects of the twelfth century were reviving the measures of that lost dynamic. Drawing out of rubble, broken archway, and severed frieze the elements necessary for reestablishing "the immutable numerical ratios of Pythagorean mysticism"—what bound, indissociably, music and architecture— they brought to bear all the basic tenets of that forgotten art for the sake of their own modus operandi.[2]

Nothing marks the influence of Roman architecture upon the Romanesque more immediately than the stonework itself. Hewn, dressed, and laid in large courses to face one facade after another, ashlar came to dominate rubblework by the beginning of the twelfth century, finally replacing it altogether in every major ecclesiastical structure. The cyclopean aspect of antique monuments— their massive blocks faced, quite often, with rusticated surfaces and jointed, one to the next, in such a manner that they required no mortar whatsoever—had clearly marked the spirits of these medieval craftsmen. As a result, a distinctly classicizing architecture arose in the lower Rhône Valley: there, that is, where Roman vestige—serving as memorabilia—was most prevalent. Characteristic of this emergent style, Romanesque basilicas in Provence can be distinguished by a somewhat stark, austere, monumental demeanor. This is due, in great part, to massive facades scarcely relieved by decorative or auxiliary elements. Aside from their entranceways facing westward, it's the discreet elegance of the stonework itself that constitutes their major embellishment. Altogether, such sobriety goes to "enhance the value of the architectural ensemble."[3]

In regard to those entranceways, one can only be struck by their marked resemblance to Roman monuments. Be it in the semicircular arches that span their portals, redolent of the antique triumphal arches in the immediate area, or the fluted columns that rise into Corinthian capitals, the capitals themselves surmounted by massive entablatures, each of these architectonic elements recalls the antique. In standing, for instance, before the magnificent entry to the Abbey of Saint-Gilles-du-Gard (Gard) or the stout countryside chapel of Saint-Gabriel (Bouches-du-Rhône) that's rung in an equally reminiscent grove of olive trees, one is witness to a *remémoration*. In sites such as these (and there are many), the Provençal Romanesque has already entered into what Jacob Burckhardt once termed the proto-Renaissance.

It should be mentioned, in passing, that there are instances in which the prevalent spirit of that age was as much recuperative as assimilative. Edifices would emerge, in certain cases, out of the antique ruins themselves. Reemploying not only the beautifully hewn ashlar that lay about like rubble but the very columns, capitals, and entablatures found in situ, medieval architects would assemble one edifice after another out of so many discrete sections. Innumerable were the abbeys, basilicas, parish churches, and countryside chapels that arose, just then, out of all that eloquent debris. By way of example, one might cite the church of Sainte-Marie et Saint-Véran at the Fontaine-de-Vaucluse, built directly over a temple to the nymphs; that of Notre-Dame la Major in Arles, over a sanctuary to the mother goddess, Cybele; or the squat little chapel of Saint-Paul near Saint-Michel-l'Observatoire (Alpes-de-Haute-Provence), situated, reputedly, over a Roman mausoleum. In each case, the antique site provided not only the emplacement, the foundation, but—in varying degrees—the very materials out of which the Romanesque edifice emerged.

Inseparable from the architecture, the sculpture that adorns these ecclesiastic monuments displays an ever-growing affinity with the classical. Indeed, it would be erroneous to separate the two, as architecture and its ornamental decor remain such integral parts one of the other in that irresistible pull toward classicism. In tracing that attraction from its inception in the eleventh century, one can distinguish several distinct periods. Each leads, inexorably, into the next. The earliest can scarcely be considered Provençal, let alone classical, in its graphic ambition. Coming as it does, though, after five centuries of silence, in which little more than a few scattered Carolingian chancel barriers attest to any sculptural activity whatsoever (see "Celestial Paradigms," p. 107 above), it marks—in its own archaic manner—an awakening. Even if the "human figures are rigid, seen either in profile or frontally," as in the bas-reliefs at Saint-Restitut (Vaucluse), and can't be considered properly articulated in an anatomical sense, one has—at least—the first attempts at figurative representation (fig. 13). No matter how static or stereotypic, the human form, here, has begun reasserting itself. Works of this order clearly emulate "late Roman and sub-Antique art overlaid with the essentially linear art of the barbarian invaders."[4] Stylistically, that is, they're modeled after relatively degenerate works that date—almost indeterminately— from the fifth to the ninth century.

Figure 13. Three figures bearing offerings, Saint-Restitut (Vaucluse). Drawing by Gabriel Sobin.

Henceforth, one can follow the emergence of an increasingly articulated human figure in Romanesque bas-relief in a more or less sequential manner. This marked evolution in time can be attributed—to a great extent—to a growing retrospection on the part of Romanesque stone sculptors. As the carved figures progressively flourish in terms of relief, suggested movement, and verisimilitude, the source of their inspiration recedes in time. Indeed, the Provençal Romanesque might be said to reach its apogee in emulating—in its most accomplished works—a pre-Christian, Greco-Roman archetype.

By way of illustration, one might compare the aforementioned bas-reliefs at Saint-Restitut, dating most likely from the eleventh century, with those executed by a certain Brunus for the portals of Saint-Gilles-du-Gard at the beginning of the twelfth century. Clearly inspired by Early Christian sarcophagi (Saint-Gilles-du-Gard is only sixteen kilometers from Arles, where such works were prominently displayed within the confines of Saint-Honorat-des-Alyscamps), the figures depicted, despite their "extraordinary archaic ruggedness," express gesture, anatomical articulation: the first stirrings, that is, of classical revival.[5] Assuming, at last, human proportions, realistic physiognomies, and distinct individual characteristics, the figures of Saint Matthew and Saint Bartholomew—even if depicted in frozen motion—celebrate the reemergence of the fully resemblant (fig. 14).

This reemergence, it should be noted, was slow in evolving. It arose, curiously enough, not with an imitation of the classical figure but with the timid replication of leaves—foliated scrolls *(rinceaux)*—discernible on antique monuments. In his comprehensive study, *Architectural Sculpture in Romanesque Provence*, Alan Borg makes a convincing argument in regard to the influence exerted on stone sculptors by the antique foliage scrolls found on Cavaillon's Arch of Marius. These scrolls served as a model not only for the frieze on Cavaillon's Notre-Dame Cathedral but for the ornament of a number of other religious edifices in the general area. At Pernes-les-Fontaines (Vaucluse), for instance, the very same Roman prototype clearly influenced the manner in which the scrolled decor of Notre-Dame-de-Nazareth was executed. There, however, "the leaves, instead of being totally flat, become slightly convex, curling inwards at the edges," writes Borg. "In this *rinceau* we can trace the beginning of the development which was to culminate in what might be termed the 'stylized naturalism' of the superb *rinceau* at S. Gilles or the acanthus capitals in the Arles cloister" (fig. 15).[6]

In what appears as little more than a series of minor academic observations, one can follow, in fact, the first initiatory moments—call it the burgeoning—of that reemergent humanism. As pod after pod, leaf after leaf, and tendril after tendril come uncurled, contour, relief, and verisimilitude reassert themselves. In short, one is

Figure 14.   Saint Matthew and Saint Bartholomew, Saint-Gilles-du-Gard
(Gard). Drawing by Gabriel Sobin.

witness, here, to the slow but irrepressible return of realistic figuration. After so many centuries of stylization, codification, and, finally, resolute suppression, the figurative—in the form of these first
tenuous foliate scrolls—comes to celebrate its own reaffirmation.

Figure 15. Rinceau at Saint-Gilles-du-Gard (Gard). Drawing by Gabriel Sobin.

Taking heart, no doubt, in this art of replication, stone sculptors began addressing the human figure with increased regard for scale, proportion, and personal characteristics. The realm of the visual had suddenly come to coincide with that of the ideated; a physical apprehension of the world, with that of the transcendent.

Even more, perhaps, than the figures found on Roman monuments, it was those carved on the aforementioned sarcophagi that served, now, as models for stone sculptors in this flourishing moment of the Romanesque. One can follow that irrepressible movement in the direction of a realistic rendering of the human form as it reverts—as already suggested—to an ever earlier source of inspiration. If the figures of Saint Matthew and Saint Bartholomew at Saint-Gilles-du-Gard were clearly inspired by representations dating from a relatively late moment in early Christian sarcophagal art, the Romanesque sculpture that immediately ensues adopts models increasingly imbued with a classicism that either antedates Christianity altogether or derives from its earliest pastoral configurations (see "Crypto-Christianity," p. 20 above). Monumental sculptures, for instance, belonging to the same facade but executed by yet other sculptors already give evidence of a far more antique appreciation of the human form. Under so much flowing drapery, the anatomy—at last—reasserts itself. In one work after another the "stiff, almost frozen attitudes give way to a gracefully rhythmic and interlocking composition."[7] Through the thin clinging pleats of the figures' costumes, knees can be seen to project, hips to pivot, and arms to extend, reclaiming a full range of gestural expressions. One is witness, indeed, to a form of figurative resuscitation. The sculptures, be they of marble or limestone, seem suddenly imbued with life, depicting figures that by their very posture, ponderation, and attitude, assume the characteristics of the living.

By the middle of the twelfth century, the influence of the Greco-Roman upon the Romanesque became evident a bit everywhere. This was especially the case in regard to the human figure, as frieze, capital, and tympanum came to receive—with a heightened sense of verisimilitude—saints and angels, prophets and apostles. Free, now, to express movement from within, these figures—simultaneously—rose markedly in relief. Taking a greater and greater distance from their underlying ground, they appear to liberate themselves from the stultifying dictates wherein *letter* had long since taken precedence over *image;* wherein "word," for centuries, had dominated "flesh." It was the latter, now, that declared itself, and—along with it—that all-confirming signature of palpable reality: the cast shadow (see "The Deletion of Shadow," p. 59 above). Swelling to the round, reoccupying as they did the third dimension, figure after figure emerged to celebrate a faith in which sacred and secular had grown indissociable.

Wind, too, entered these rife iconographies. Tugging at the stone garments, say, of some blessed figure, wind served to animate that figure from without. Rippling, for instance, through

Figure 16.   Rope-puller in a frieze at Saint-
Paul-les-Trois-Châteaux (Drôme). Drawing by
Gabriel Sobin.

the mantle of the Virgin Mary or puffing in *plis soufflés* about the
ankles of Saint Jerome, it brought the air—the very world—to
play about this once stolid, immutable statuary. Suddenly, all's
astir, alive (fig. 16). In emulating the aesthetics of a classicism that
had been refuted nearly a thousand years earlier, in progressing
but only to the extent that it resuscitated, the Romanesque
reached full maturity. Tapping a seemingly extinct resource, it
managed—by the mid-twelfth century—to draw forth all the
nourishment it needed to depict a fresh, fully reinvigorated, vision of existence. Out of classical roots would thus spring an
abundance of evangelical branches.

Vanished Scaffolds and the Structures Thereof

for Jean-Marie Chiappa, bâtisseur

Every Romanesque edifice had its double: its ephemeral counterpart. Rising at exactly the same rate as the edifice, the scaffolding—a makeshift arrangement of boards, tie-beams, and matted branches—would vanish once the structure itself reached completion. Indispensable to its edification, the scaffolding became—at that very moment—obsolete. It left nothing as memento but, occasionally, a smattering of small, usually square, sockets embedded within the completed structure. Called putlog holes, these sockets or slots served to anchor the putlog—a short horizontal timber on which the scaffold rested—fast to the wall under construction. They were, indeed, the point of juncture between structure and counterstructure, between the solid stone edifice and those rickety wood assemblages that went into its consolidation.

Today these putlog holes stud the facades of any number of Romanesque buildings. Whether in isolated sections or aligned in

Figure 17.   The chapel Sainte-Madeleine at Mirabeau
(Vaucluse). The putlog holes embedded in the facade indicate
the emplacement of the original scaffolding. These are not to be
confused with the pigeon holes over the oculus in this chapel-
cum-dovecote. Photo by the author.

vertical or horizontal rows, they may be read like stray notes belonging to a sheet of lost medieval music. Interpreted by both historians and archeologists of the vertical, they allow one a surprising glimpse into that vanished world. Even better, in deciphering the traces inscribed within the masonry itself, one can begin reconstituting—pole after pole, plank after plank—the overall structure of those otherwise evanescent assemblages. The notes, no matter how stray, serve as indices—punctual, precise—to entire sequences of that lost medieval composition.

"Once the construction reached shoulder-height," writes one historian, "the mason would employ provisional wood structures in order to reach different levels of the edifice, be it to build, consolidate, or repair."[1] Scaffoldings could be either freestanding (laid flush, that is, against a given surface) or embedded, creating thereby those unmistakable sockets in the predominantly uniform facades. The putlog holes, in turn, could be either masoned (wherein a lintel, jambs, and an underlying support would be provided) or dressed (wherein a hole would be carved within a hewn block of coursed masonry). Either way, a rhythm—a visual resonance—would be introduced into the blind facade that certain medievalists consider not only functional but, perhaps, deliberately decorative.

A putlog hole is nearly always situated at the intersection of a given course of horizontal stonework and a vertical standard, or scaffolding pole. It can thus be read—interpreted—in relation to these two determinants. Of the two, however, it's far easier to trace its horizontal or lateral alignment, for it often varies little more than the width of a single overlapping floorboard. This slight variant— solidly inscribed within the masonry as much as a thousand years earlier—reveals a momentary expedient on some mason's part.

For the boards needed to overlap in order to scaffold a broad un-broken expanse. There, the raised note of the putlog hole testifies to such an arrangement. Far greater divergences often exist, how-ever, in a lateral reading of such holes, especially when the facade is subdivided by pilaster strips or buttresses. In such instances, the scaffolding is erected in the interval between such supports and can only be interpreted within a context of so many discrete units. One must also take into account work sites that underwent, over the years, a succession of building campaigns. Each of these cam-paigns would have necessitated a fresh set of scaffoldings. In such cases, the putlog holes often take on entirely new alignments, as if, quite suddenly, they were describing notes to an entirely new music. As indices, they've helped scholars reconstitute the often complex history of a given medieval structure.

On certain facades, one occasionally detects a pair of discrete putlog holes situated entirely by themselves in parallel opposition. Often located on either side of a tympanum or oculus, these holes once anchored a twin-pronged cantilevered scaffold in place. This small mobile structure would be employed whenever some com-plicated ornament—whether in carved stone or leaded glass—needed to be installed. Spanning a relatively short distance, it in-variably bracketed an area demanding particular attention.

A vertical interpretation of these square sockets (averaging ten to fifteen centimeters on each side) often proves harder to esta-blish than a lateral one. For their vertical alignment entirely de-pended on the disposition of the scaffolding poles that they once served to anchor. Most especially, it depended on how those poles were lashed one to the next as the scaffolding rose the full height of the edifice. Today, in reading these scored walls, one can in-terpret the vertical arrangement of the putlog holes in any one of the following ways (fig. 18): in pure alignment, where the holes rise uninterruptedly along one side of the same pole; in monoaxial alternation, where the holes are aligned upon alternating sides of the same pole; in external alternation, where the holes are aligned on opposite sides of two poles ligated end-to-end and thus separated by the very width that those two poles occupy; in diaxial displacement, where the holes, located on each side of those two ligated uprights, lie separated by the width of only one of them; and in internal alternation, where the holes, once again, lie on either side of each upright but, in facing inward, enjoy the same interval as the foregoing: i.e., that of a single width.[2]

Out of so much apparent irregularity, perfectly coherent compositions can often be detected, interpolated. For the deeply embedded notes that punctuate these Romanesque structures are never fortuitous. They originally belonged to a plan, a pattern, no matter how ephemeral. Patiently examined, they allow one, today, enough indices to reconstitute their long vanished assemblages. The putlog holes alone will indicate—for instance—that the platforms they once served to support were often placed at intervals no more than a meter high, requiring masons to work in an exceedingly stooped position. Alongside them, one can readily imagine, lay an array of trowels, spatulas, plumb lines and T squares, not to mention troughs full of freshly prepared mortar and blocks of quarried stone that the masons were in the process, just then, of bedding. Alongside them, porters, foremen (*maîtres d'œuvre*), even the architects themselves, would crowd into these cramped makeshift quarters. Below, at ground level, stonecutters (*lapicides*) would be dressing fresh blocks, communicating *viva voce* with the masons overhead as to a stone's proper dimensions or the exact emplacement for a putlog hole in a given bit of ashlar.

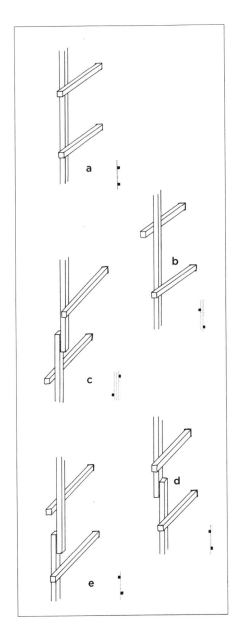

Figure 18. Distribution of putlog holes in relation to five distinct forms of scaffolding: (a) pure alignment; (b) monoaxial alternation; (c) external alternation; (d) diaxial displacement; (e) internal alternation. Drawing by Ghislaine Macabeo (© ALPARA, *DARA* no. 13).

Finally, one might add to this brief reconstitution a network of ladders leading from one platform to the next; an array of pulleys, winches, cords; and, as a kind of masthead, high over the entire crosshatched structure, the topmost scaffold pole sporting the heraldic pennant of the *commanditaire* himself.

There is, then—in all this—a music to be read. The putlog holes alone furnish the score for any number of otherwise long-lost compositions. That music belongs, if anywhere, to a world of antecedents, to that elaborate sine qua non that both precedes and accompanies each and every act of invention, creation, accomplishment. Wood against stone, the evanescent against the ever-lasting, it went to determine—over and over—the magnificence of Romanesque architecture. Be it at Conques, Saint-Michel-de-Cuxa, or—quite simply—alongside the flanks of some abandoned chapel high in the Languedocian moorlands, it prepared the facing edifice for all posterity. This music, in fact, is that of attune-ments. Fragile, self-eradicating, it can only be heard; and, heard, fully appreciated as a music played out in anticipation of the masterpiece to come.

~✦~

Incastellamento

Perching the Village, I

The following essay attempts to place the emergence of the medieval perched village within a long-standing geohistorical perspective.

In the foothills of southeastern France, one can readily interpret history—the history of human habitat, at least—on altitude alone. One can go, for instance, from Paleolithic caves and rock overhangs to the earliest open-air sites of the Neolithic, immediately below. In dropping, say, forty, fifty meters, one may climb down out of the desolate shelters of an ice age culture, based essentially on predation, and arrive at the faint but unmistakable traces of the first food-producing societies in the richly tilled plains beneath. Indeed, bits of their thatched-roof, cobbed-wall dwellings are still detectable today, embossed in negative upon the abundant potsherds scattered about the earth's surface. From the Paleolithic to the Neolithic, then—from a glacial environment to an essentially temperate one—the culturally curious can journey downward as if on an invisible ladder: that of human accommodation itself.

This ladder, one comes to realize, serves as an index of sorts. For the altitude at which a particular society inhabited helps indicate the pressures—be they climatic or socioeconomic—to which that society was exposed, and the manner in which it adjusted or succumbed to those pressures at any given historical moment. In the quintessential shift, say, from the Paleolithic to the Neolithic—entirely determined by climatic conditions—one has a perfect example of such an adjustment. Populations no longer needed to huddle in rock shelters against the cold of a glacial environment. To the contrary, as the glaciers retracted, followed by the slow yet inexorable advent of agriculture, those populations could settle directly alongside the fields they would till, sow, and harvest. Evidence of that critical transformation is manifest everywhere. One still finds polished stone axes used at that time for clearing the surrounding wilderness, and flint blades glistening with sickle gloss: a transparent deposit of silica found along the blade's edge from having gleaned—year after year—those earliest domesticated cereal grasses.

This first hesitant, yet all-determinant appropriation of natural resources would have overwhelming consequences. Not the least of those consequences would be the emergence of warfare for the first time in human history. As populations rose throughout the Neolithic, so would a nascent sense of territory. Bit by bit, boundary disputes would lead to open conflict. Archeological evidence has revealed, for instance, a disproportionate increase in flint weaponry in relation to game species remainders found in home sites. This growing differential could have but one cause. Indeed, signs of tension and open hostility between Neolithic communities rise at much the same rate as their growing reclamation of the surrounding wilderness. As more and more land was required to nourish an ever-expanding population, these territorial disputes would increase in both number and virulence. In an early attempt at marking territorial limits, these late Neolithic societies began constructing dolmens—their collective chamber tombs—along ridges, raised promontories: sites visible, that is, from a considerable distance. Venerated from within, they also served to lay a *cordon sanitaire* about a prescribed area, thereby warning any would-be invaders. This protective tissue, however, was easily pierced. As needs became greater, so did encroachment. Finally, these plains people, living and working in richly irrigated regions and exposed, therefore, to invasion, began moving upland. Seeking shelter in the surrounding hillsides, they settled upon rock outcrops, counterforts, natural acropoli. This movement would, most likely, mark the first migration in history of a population reacting to socioeconomic pressures in a topographically vertical manner, given that such pressures had probably never before existed. Hesitant at first, this movement upland would increase dramatically with the arrival of metals: of bronze and, soon after, iron. While warrior cultures, predominantly Celtic, arrived out of the northeast, and maritime cultures— Phoenician, Etruscan, and finally Greek—established trading posts along the coastline to the south, these hill communities, undergoing both assimilation and acculturation, were converted into Iron Age fortresses. Constituting so-called microstates, these *oppida* rung in moats, wooden palisades, and concentric rings of massive drystone ramparts would contain—for the first time in human history—the stocked storage jars and silos of a surplus economy. Having gone from subsistence farming on the plains to this surplus production in perched settlements, Iron Age societies had entered, de facto, an economy based on deferment, speculation, trade. The *oppida*, consequently, became not only habitats but granaries, warehouses, and banks.

This civilization of *oppida*, as it came to be called, was what Caesar discovered upon entering Gaul. He immediately realized that these hill fortresses had to be subdued and dismantled if he were to control that vast region. Otherwise, the *oppida* themselves would continue commanding not only the hinterland above but the trade routes and riverways immediately beneath. Caesar, issuing an injunction of no more than four words, ordered the hill populations to abandon their fortresses and settle in the plains below. "Caesar in planum deduxit," he proclaimed.[1] Those who obeyed this dictate were allotted fertile tracts of land in the valleys; those who refused saw their fortresses stormed and destroyed, their lives and livelihood reduced to one of pure destitution.

Here again, one has an eloquent example of history acting upon altitude—and altitude, upon history—in terms of human habitation. One can travel down that invisible ladder, descend from any one of hundreds of ruined *oppida* in Provence, still rife with Iron Age ceramics, and enter the heavily romanized plains below. Here, too, one can not only wander through Roman cities such as Orange, Vaison-la-Romaine, Arles, and Nîmes; not only travel over Roman roads and cross any one of several stalwart Roman bridges; but enjoy a landscape that—in many cases—was laid out by Roman land surveyors in an unending succession of square centuriations (approximately 710 meters on each side). At no point, however, does one leave the fertile plains, for at no point, in fact, would that far-reaching, colonizing civilization settle but at an altitude low enough and in sites accessible enough to assure total control.

And so, for nearly three centuries running, Gallo-Roman *Provincia* would thrive as essentially a plains civilization. Throughout that time, people dwelled either in cities *(civitatis)* or in the countryside, be it in *villae*—country estates with agricultural dependencies inhabited by all-powerful landlords, their families, and a servile workforce—or in *vici*, improvised villages often located, significantly enough, at the base of abandoned *oppida*. There, communities would languish in the shadow of their deserted hill fortresses directly overhead, such as those who inhabited the hamlet of Mananqua beneath the *oppidum* of Ménerbes or that of the Grande Bastide beneath Buoux.

With the first wave of barbaric invasions, however, the stability of the *pax Romana* began giving way. From 260 onward, Provence was subject to a seemingly endless series of raids, devastations, and successor state occupations that would undermine civic order and finally leave the once flourishing Gallo-Roman cities and country estates in ruin. The populations, in response, fled. Those, at least, who didn't take shelter in the lee of ramparts or in the barricaded arcades of deserted arenas fled in the one direction that human instinct had invariably dictated: upward. For altitude, throughout history, has always spelled refuge, security. In times of distress, if not outright terror, it's toward those rock escarpments that the distraught have infallibly turned. And turn they did. Throughout the Dark Ages, they either constructed drystone hovels—*bories*—at a certain altitude or returned to the ruined *oppida* themselves. There, in those hill citadels that their distant ancestors had been forced to abandon centuries earlier, these communities didn't so much reconstruct as reassemble whatever dilapidated structures still remained. Living on a day-to-day basis in a hand-to-mouth manner, they reinforced ramparts and, occasionally, erected wooden watchtowers *(turris specula)*. Otherwise, it was a time marked by makeshift arrangements and pure fortuity that left little or no written trace of itself: a period of historiographic eclipse (see "The Dark Ages: A History of Omissions," p. 85 above). Within the diocese of Apt alone, even the episcopal records (the only ones kept throughout the early Middle Ages) ceased to exist for two-and-a-half centuries, and there is every evidence that the bishops themselves, under the prevailing terror, became itinerant, moving through the ruins of their own devastated estates or taking refuge in one perched settlement after another.

It can be said, in fact, that for nearly five full centuries—from the sixth to the eleventh—the better part of the population either lived or took recurrent shelter at altitude. "For the mountains," in Fernand Benoît's words, "had become the repository of both the people and their traditions."[2] Those perched abodes—rude, austere, precarious—would preserve, nonetheless, what had been routed, extirpated from the once lavish plains below. Unwritten, unrecorded, the memory of a lost order would lie—at those heights—as if dormant. Like some kind of mnemonic tuber, it would await—within the paucity of that terrain—its moment. It wasn't until the summer of 973, however, that that moment finally arrived. A monk, descendant of one of Provence's ruling families and destined, by his fervor, for sainthood, had been taken prisoner by Saracens and placed in irons. Overnight, Mayeul's capture became a rallying call for a still obscure Provençal aristocracy. Chasing the Saracens from their mountain retreats and liberating, in the process, Mayeul himself, they inadvertently set into play a series of events that would lead to that "first renaissance," as the Romanesque has frequently been called. For they'd discovered by this very action a community of interests and an unsuspected power long since monopolized by the bishops. Within less than two years, they began constructing small fortified strongholds against the common enemy. These structures, situated at a certain altitude, lay related to one another by a tight network of political affiliations. By swearing oaths of allegiance, the lords of those tiny manors quite unwittingly inaugurated a form of feudalism that would last for centuries to come.

These strongholds, or *castra* (signifying in Latin fortified sites or fortresses), took the form of tiny keeps armed with archers' loopholes or, occasionally, of clustered dwellings circumscribed by ramparts *(circuitus castri)*. In either case, these structures tend to astonish the present-day visitor by their sheer modesty. Behind walls that can reach a depth of two full meters will lie some minuscule chamber or dwarflike courtyard no more than twenty meters square. Indeed, these first stalwart constructions, coming as they did in a sudden, unexpected resurgence of creative energies, impress more by their solidity than their size. After five consecutive centuries of devastation that sent entire populations scurrying across wasteland to settle in whatever makeshift quarters they could find for themselves, these *castra* celebrate—no matter how seignorial in context—a newfound sense of security, confidence, and general well-being.

At this point, however, history—that unpredictable sequence of preestablished determinants—appears to enter into contradiction even with itself. For no sooner was that first wave of construction underway, assuring a tentative defense system against the Saracen invader, than the Saracens were expelled not only from Provence but from the continent itself. The Age of Invasions had come to an end. Curiously enough, though, construction—at this given moment—didn't abate so much as accelerate. Against no given enemy, ramparts, palisades, bastions, and watchtowers—the whole panoply of military architecture—flourished. One after another, hilltops were capped in castles and became—with the advent of the new millennium—ever more imposing, self-assertive. As the architectural translation of aristocratic power, they symbolized the sudden emergence of local dynasties. Arising out of total obscurity or some loose, often fallacious, claim to Carolingian ancestry, these dynasties established—by the construction of those very *castra*—zones of influence that would radiate outward across the landscape. More and more divided and subdivided, that surrounding landscape would find itself increasingly partitioned into discrete units. Indeed, between the edification of those first castles and the subdivision of the surrounding landscape, the physiognomy of present-day Provence was—grosso modo—being determined.

As the *castra* grew in size throughout the eleventh century, so would the number of houses, or dependencies, clustered about their base. Whole villages, now—wrapped helicoidal—would rise in narrowing spirals toward the all-dominant pinnacles overhead. This process, called *incastellamento* by historians, involved a massive resettling of the rural population within these elevated sites, along with all the attendant transformations—social, political, or psychological—that such a movement invariably entailed.[3] Out of the profound shadows of the Dark Ages, the medieval perched village—solid, self-enveloping—had, at last, emerged. Even more, as populations settled behind the security of its crenellated ramparts and began to cultivate the now pacified countryside, the very face of Europe—bit by bit—began to assert itself. Here, in prototype, lay the model for that vast medieval enterprise: the feudal state as it emerged in a profusion of locally based, semiautonomous power structures.

By the twelfth century, the *castra*, having grown both in size and number, came to be described as *castelli* in the episcopal record. These *castelli*—full-blown castles, now, usually square in plan and containing an inner courtyard—take on a seemingly contradictory character. As their defense systems grow more and more massive, impregnable, the accoutrements of leisure become more and more manifest. Windows, for instance, grow taller and wider as the space allocated for fanfare and festivities increases proportionately. Fraught with ambivalence, these masterpieces of military architecture—the very castles, indeed, that stud the hilltops of Provence today—were constructed, in fact, during a period of relative peace. Against whom, then, had their moats been dug, their drawbridges lifted, their battlements erected if not against themselves? If not against the eventuality of some unforeseeable breakdown in a delicate, altogether labyrinthian set of mutual alliances, one with the other?

Had history, here, broken pattern? Shifted ground? For hadn't abundance, well-being, the overflowing horn of a cornucopian existence always been associated with the plains below, and fear, flight, refuge, with those raised promontories, rocky counterforts, above? At this precise moment in history, however, the locus of privilege literally rose, came to associate itself with altitude. It did so not less as a defensive measure against an active enemy (as Iron Age communities had in constructing their *oppida*) than as a deliberate attempt to display and, in displaying, exercise power from above. As such, this emergent aristocracy was creating— upon so many rock outcrops—a vertical hierarchy wherein a geographical determinant would be placed in the service of a sociopolitical ambition.

Today, such a revalorization scarcely surprises. Having journeyed through history upon that invisible ladder, one finally arrives—in castles such as these—at an all-too-familiar rung: the very last. Living oneself in a world of towers, turrets, and skyscrapers, in a world marked by an ever-increasing appropriation of a once theophanic dimension, one realizes—even here, among these windblown ruins—that the past, no matter how remote, is but the precondition for the present. That stone after stone, incremental layer after incremental layer, one's own existential moment has long been in preparation. That history, in surroundings such as these—among the dilapidated monuments, that is, of the self-aggrandized—not only reveals, it foreshadows.

Incastellamento

Perching the Village, II
The *Circulades* of Languedoc

Ideally, one should be able to read passages in history at an accelerated rate: watch them evolve before one's eyes, as one might, say, a blossom bursting forth from its calyx in stop-motion cinematography. Only then, perhaps, could one begin to apprehend history as a single, singular organism, developing, flourishing, degenerating—despite the complexity of its parts—in obedience to a perfectly coherent set of causal factors.

Such would be the case, for instance, in examining the emergence of certain medieval villages in the Languedoc. For they virtually bud out of their own deep-seated historic determinants at more or less the same moment in time: the turn of the millennium. Populations that had been scattered throughout the countryside for the duration of the Dark Ages, subsisting as best they could throughout that long, desolate night, began gathering, a century before the second millennium, about churchyards, cemeteries, the abandoned *villae* of late Roman antiquity, or the first wooden keeps and strongholds *(donjons)* that were starting to speckle the rural landscape. But this first precocious movement, belonging to the false spring of the Carolingian, was—essentially—illusory, ephemeral. It would have to await the millennium and the propitious sociopolitical climate of an emergent feudalism to sprout—at long last—into what has come to be called *incastellamento:* the construction of solid fortified strongholds and the gathering of populations about them. Around the raised ground of the stronghold itself (whether on a rock outcrop or an artificial earthen motte), protovillages began radiating outward, following—quite often—a perfectly coherent, preconceived site plan. Many of these protovillages, especially those located on the level plains, would emerge *ex nihilo* in ring after ring of concentric circles. If the *castrum* in such communities might be said to represent the corolla or inner whorl, the houses in the subcastral zone (circumscribed by both streets and, infallibly, ramparts) might be seen as the calyx or outer whorl of this radiant architectural organism. In the morphogenesis of these medieval villages, each part entered, now, into an inextricable relationship with every other.

"For a village to come into being," wrote Robert Fossier, "the ground upon which its houses and public spaces are laid out must be properly allocated in relation to viable passageways and within well-recognized limits."[1] Over and over, such requisites were being met as not only the Languedoc but much of Europe emerged at this very moment out of five centuries of silence, stasis, and devastation. One can follow the growth—the efflorescence—of such villages by simply tracing the value given in medieval cartularies to the word *castrum* itself. If at first it designated exclusively the keep, the stronghold alone, it soon would signify the amalgamation of both keep and collective habitat: the castle and the now-burgeoning village that nestled against its fortifications. By the twelfth century, however, *castrum* would designate the whole village: a community that possessed fortifications. By then, a village, or outer whorl, would have taken both political and military precedence over its instigating center, the *castrum* itself.

How, though, would such a village have appeared at the outset: at the heart, that is, of what historians have called the castral revolution? At its center, of course, and upon a raised platform, would lie the castle itself. Usually built in the round for the sake of an all-commanding overview of a potential invader, it rose with little more, at first, than narrow loopholes—archers' slots—for fenestration. Here, in the *caput castri*, lived the feudal lord, his family, and the vassals who'd sworn lifelong allegiance to his person. The castle would usually be rung in moats *(fosse)*, ramparts *(muros)*, and embankments *(ager)*. Today, in a town such as Alaigne (Aude), the very names of the streets that lie in concentric order about the Place de l'Ancien Château bear witness to those original functions: Promenade des Fossés, Rue des Ramparts, Chemin de Ronde. Within these defensive structures, a first circle of habitations would envelop the castle in its ringlike concrescence. Here, in these so-called protovillages, would live artisans, peasants, and the whole human support system for the castle overhead. Beyond this original ring, yet other rings of habitations would form, each of them concentric to the last and separated, upon occasion, by second, even third, sets of intervening moats, ramparts, and embankments. The last of these defensive structures would—in turn—circumscribe the totality of the community. Immediately beyond, the agglomeration would be "aureoled in a horticultural ring":[2] those readily accessible vegetable and herbal gardens so assiduously cultivated throughout the medieval. These, finally, would give way to the *ager* proper: the orchards, vineyards, and grainfields that, on occasion, would assume the very same concentric outlines, as if they, too, had blossomed out of the calyx of the all-instigating *castrum*.

Even if hill villages couldn't always enjoy such rigorously circular ground plans, owing to their irregular relief, many still managed to form into crescent-, fan-, or oval-shaped agglomerations. Whether on the plains or foothills, however, these early preconceived microstructures, emerging at the dawn of a unified European consciousness, celebrated not only the rebirth of urbanism but—far more—a newfound confidence in community itself. Some historians, and not the least, have suggested that these Languedocian *castra* might have gone to inspire the Cathari by the sheer geometric harmony of their architectural programs.[3] Soon to be prevalent throughout that region, the Cathari would espouse a vision of tight-knit communities in which a veritable "peace on earth" might be achieved.

Whether the *universalis castri* had such a direct influence on the Cathari or not, one can't help but feel, in visiting castral villages today, an unmistakable sense that they were originally conceived as the fervent expression of some underlying human covenant. Despite whatever differences might have existed in a feudal society dominated by a rigidly codified social order, there remains— inscribed within the masonry itself—the material manifestation of a perfectly immaterial confidence in human community. The volumes not only fit, they overlap, interlock, penetrate, and relieve one another with an unfailing sense of the contiguous. All things interrelate, one with the other. Stone against stone, rooftop

Figure 19. *Circulade* of Bram (Aude). Photo courtesy of Krzysztof Pawlowski, author of *Circulades languedociennes en l'an mille* (Montpellier: Presses du Languedoc, 1992).

against rooftop, battlement against battlement: not a single element doesn't go to substantiate these cogent, all-encompassing ensembles (fig. 19).

How, then, did something so integrated, so organically interdependent, come undone? Emerging at the turn of the millennium and reaching a peak in the first half of the twelfth century, these self-enclosed, self-sustaining, protourban structures began to lose their raison d'être toward the end of the twelfth or beginning of the thirteenth century. At that time, a major innovation in military architecture transferred the central defense system of the *castrum* from the stronghold—located on its motte, or rock outcrop, at the village's very heart—to the last outlying rampart.

Decentralization had already begun. Then, too, as the numerous internecine struggles common to the eleventh and twelfth centuries subsided, so would the need to huddle behind high ramparts in the shadow of some stalwart castle. By the fourteenth century, many of these encastellated villages—especially those located on perched sites in relatively inaccessible regions—were completely abandoned, while others broke symmetry altogether and appear to have poured out into the surrounding countryside in the absence, now, of any cohesive, interrelated structure whatsoever. As to the populations themselves, many had begun moving into the cities as an entirely new set of material circumstances—sociopolitical, economic, or military—came into play. *Incastellamento* had clearly served its time.

Today, in visiting any one of these fossilized villages, be it some windswept ruin in the hinterlands, massively invaded each summer by tourists, or some modernized *commune* on the plains—its original radioconcentric site plan virtually choked by the convulsive growth of its surrounding suburbs—one ineluctably thinks of Yeats. "Things fall apart," he wrote in "The Second Coming," "the centre cannot hold." Throughout the medieval, the center, idyllically conceived as the terrestrial reflection of a celestial order—bound human societies to a divinely inspired vision of existence. "Such symbolism," writes William Alexander McClung, "is utopian as well as cosmological in Plato's imaginary cities, those of the *Laws*, where the town is circular, and of the *Timaeus* and the *Critias*, where, in the layout of Atlantis, square and circle are juxtaposed. St. Augustine understood the circle as a symbol of virtue and anagogically representative of virtue 'because of the conformity and concordance of its essentials.' "[4] Nowhere is such circularity more apparent in medieval iconography than in the image of God Himself as architect of the universe. Compass in hand, He lays out his creation in the form of a perfect circle (fig. 20). Then, too, images of Jerusalem—the circular city par excellence in the popular imagination—proliferated around this time (fig. 21). These images served as archetypal models for any number of millennial communities yet in construction.

Such a vision, of course, has long since vanished. And if one could benefit from that accelerated cinematographic overview suggested at the outset of this essay, one would be free to follow that original mineral blossom as it broke inexorably into a plethora of incoherent parts. Faubourgs, then suburbs, then outlying *zones industrielles,* obeying no law other than that of personal whim or corporate expedience, have long since violated those perfectly organic, self-enveloping ensembles. As for the castles, located at their center, most have vanished altogether. In certain cases, they've been replaced by an oversized Gothic church (Lasbordes, in the Aude), a latter-day Disneyesque castle (Margon, in the Hérault), or some presumptuous nineteenth-century city hall (Frontignan, also in the Hérault). In yet others, a cement water tower (Mauguio) or a monument to the dead of the First World War (Abeilhan—both in the Hérault) caps an empty earthen platform on which once stood—perfectly centripetal—some stout medieval fortress. Then, too, one might find nothing whatsoever, today, but an empty square, a ring of houses circumscribing an historic void. In villages such as Donazac, Alaigne, and La Force (all in the Aude), one is confronted, indeed, with a spectacle of pure vacuity. Nothing remains of their *castra:* those nuclei about which entire communities not only clustered but thrived in a tight network of reciprocities, of mutual interdependencies. One is likely to find, in their place, little more than a parking lot or a

Figure 20. God the Father measuring the universe, from the *Bible moralisée* (probably Reims, mid-thirteenth century). Österreichischen Nationalbibliothek, Vienna, cod. 2554, fol. 1v (© Erich Lessing / Art Resource, NY).

Ierosolima nomē vrbis in palestina me tropolis iudeoȝ:pȝiꝰ Iebꝰ.postea salē. tercio bierosolima. vltio belia dicta. Cu ius vrbis pȝiūꝰ ꝺditoȝ fuit(vt Iosephꝰ testat) Canaan q iust appellat erat rex. Et b qꝺē mel cbisedecb sacerdos ꝺei altissimi dicebatur. Qui cū ibidē pbanū edificass illud Solimā appella uit.solimi fuerūt pplī iuxta liciā q̃s bomerꝰ pui gnatissimos:ꝛ a belleropbōte ꝺeuictos dicit. et in mōubꝰbitasse. Et corneliꝰ tacit cū ꝺe iudeoȝ origine opionē narrat ait. Alij clara iudeoȝ iniꝶ tia solimos carmibꝰ celebratā bomeri gentē ꝺꝺi tam vrbē bierosolimā noīe suo fecisse. vn Iuue nalis interpres legū solimaȝ. q̃ ciuitas cananee gentis vsꝗ ad tpa ꝺauid regī bitatio fuit. Nec so lue iudeoȝ priceps eos cananeos seu iebuseos expellere potuit. Dauid iebuseis expulsis cū ci uitatem reedificasset eā bierosolimā.r. munitissi mā nūcupauit. Ibuiꝰ vrb situs ꝛ munitio petro sa erat. ꝛ triplici muro cingebatur. q̃ vt Sirabo ait inter a̾q̃s abundans exten vo olio siccam fossam bēbat i lapide erasam.xl. pedū ꝑfundiꝶ tate. latituꝺo vo.cc.l. Elapide aūt eraso educta erant celeberrimi tepli menia. Ꝧec bierosolima lōge clarissima vrbium orientis sup ꝺuos colles erat ꝺdita iteruallo ꝺiscretos i quā ꝺōꝰ arcberrime ꝺesinebāt. Collū alter q̃ supior citas excelꝶ sioȝ ꝛ i.plixtate ꝺirectioȝ castellu ꝺauid dicebaꝶ tur. Alter q̃ iseriorē sustinet citates vndiꝗ ꝺecliꝶ uius ē vall'i medio ad syloā ꝑtins ita fōtē q̃ ꝺulcē ē vocabāt. firmissime ā̾t ꝺō salomōis aliorūꝗ i

terra regū opa oȝnata fuit. agrippa eꝰ ptes citatī addiderat ꝛ cinꝶerat. Exuberās essm mīlituꝺine paulati extra menia sꝑebāt. Ꝧoiata ē ꝗs addiꝶ ta noua citas. Offnē ā̾t citatī i giro spaciū.xxx.ꝛ mbꝰ stadijs sinieba̾t. Et si i toto aꝺmirabis. ter cius murꝰ aꝺmirabilioȝ ob excellētias turrī q̃ ad septētrionē occidētēꝗ surgebat i agulo. ꝺe q̃ soꝶ le oȝto arabia .ꝑspici poterat ꝛ mare vsꝗ ad siꝶ nes bebȝeoȝ. Et iuxta eā turrī yppico:ꝛ ꝺue q̃s berodes i ātiq̃ muro edificauerat. Mirabil fuit lapidū magnituꝺo ex secto marmore cādiꝺo ita aꝺuāt vt single turres singla saxa viꝺeȝē. bꝰis i septētriōali pte aula ꝛgia pʃāstissima ꝺiūgebaꝶ tur. Muro alto cincta acꝶ arietate saxoȝū oȝnata dbᷓte ꝺeniꝗ porticꝰ ꝑ carclm flexe coliūeꝗ i siꝶ gulis:q̃ iter eas sb ꝺiuo parebāt spacia vbi erāt viriꝺaria cū asternis eneis. qbꝰ aq̃ effundebaꝶt. ꝑudet dicere b ꝛgia q̃ī fuerat cū slāma ab itestiꝶ nis isidiatoribꝰ oīa sumpsit. De excidio tn bꝰ regie vrb isenꝰ patebit: vrbē aū̾t sacras reddidit moȝs xpī. ꝑlaꝗs saꝶc i eo loco viꝺere possumus Amnē. s.q̃ lotꝰē xpꝰs. Teplū seu tepli ruinas i q̃ wait. locāybi cū ssima bū̾litate passus ē corpe vt nos aī passionibꝰ libaret. sepulcȝ vbi sactississ mū illō corpꝰ ꝶbstitit. Et vn ascediit in celū. q̃ ad iudicāū fuerisꝶē creꝺit. vbi vetꝛꝛ sluncbꝰ ipauit vbi ꝺeixꝗ elegit iꝺoctos atꝗ iopes piscatoȝes. q̃s rū bamis ꝛ rbenbꝰpiscareī ipatoȝes ꝛ ꝛges gēꝶ tius. vbi cecos illīiauit. leptosos mūdauit. paꝶ raliticos erexit. moȝuos suscitauit. Multaꝗ̾ alia q̃ lōge psed teꝺiosū eēt. cū ex euāge. nō sint

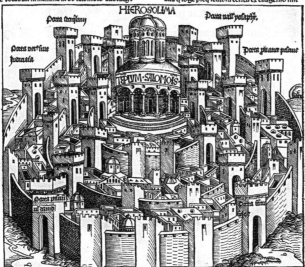

HIEROSOLIMA

TEPLVM · SALOMOIS

Porta trasliuy   Porta vall'iosapbat.

Porta vet'siue   Porta pisane pinue
iudiuata

Porta piluii   Porta aūr
ul auud   kator

Figure 21.   Jerusalem as a *circulade*, from a woodcut in Hartman Schedel's *Liber Chronicarum* (Nuremberg, 1493). Gift of Tamar and Teddy Kollek, The Israel Museum, Jerusalem (photo © The Israel Museum).

dusty circle in which a few old men—in bleached blue work jackets—pass the time playing *boules.*

Certainly, one can feel nostalgia for worlds never known, for orders—whether aesthetic, sociopolitical, or transcendent—never previously encountered. This, in fact, might be the lesson one can draw from these Languedocian *circulades,* as they've come to be called. They awaken one to an underlying human disposition that might otherwise have gone totally ignored. Read at speed, in cinematographic stop-motion, they blossom, flourish, and then break into incoherent patterns, satisfying socially deconstructed needs. One has watched them, in short, wilt, decompose. They've left, however, enough evidence of their original geometries at the heart of any number of present-day *communes* to allow one to read—reconstitute—their history not only forward, in "regressive evolution," but backward, toward the very instant of their inception.[5] Doing so, one is struck, today, in entering any of these medieval sites, by the *architectural resonance* emitted out of so many successive concentric circles. For it's this aura, finally, this effluence of a once radial community that remains—notwithstanding centuries of dereliction, obsolescence, and indifference—perfectly ineffaceable.

꒰ꜱ꒱

Faja Oscura

The rupture in biological equilibrium between man and the
forest over the past eight thousand years has nearly reached
its conclusion.

Aline Durand

The historian, scurrying after the charged particles of history that
lie scattered across landscape, has become the avid collector of an
ever-expanding wealth of residue, vestige, and substantiating evidence. As modern methods of detection grow more and more re-
fined, that very evidence dramatically increases. Whole medieval
forests, for example, have come to light through the minuscule eye-
piece of some palynologist's microscope. Not only pollen fossil but
wood charcoal—called "the memory of the forest" by one
specialist—undergoes exacting analysis.[1] These two indices, extracted from their own vestigial milieu, help modern-day historians reconstitute—with stunning accuracy—the life of those long-
vanished forests. Their findings over the past decades have proved
increasingly informative. For they help clarify not only a crucial

aspect of medieval history but a pivotal moment in humanity's interrelation with nature.

That interrelation was slow in evolving. Beginning seven thousand years earlier, with the arrival of the Neolithic in the western Mediterranean (circa 5000 B.C.), the first spoliations of the forest floor must have been relatively slight. Agropastoral societies began clearing ground at the forest's edge for pasture, employing their hafted stone axe heads to do so. With the arrival of metals, however (bronze at about 2000 B.C., iron at about 700 B.C.), there is a sudden acceleration in this process of deforestation. Not only do metal axe heads prove far more efficacious in felling trees, but recent pollen analyses have attested to the sudden widespread use of fire, as well, for clearing woodlands. The otherwise inexplicable emergence of eagle fern and birch wood, as revealed by these analyses—plants which thrive in a markedly calcinated milieu—testify to the growing use, at this time, of slash-and-burn techniques.

The forest would undergo further incursions with the arrival of the Romans in the first century B.C. Protoindustrial, they needed vast quantities of wood for smelting metals, calcining lime, blowing glass, and firing bricks and tiles, not to mention all the beams, floorboards, pillars and pilotis required for construction. One can safely say that in the tripart division of the natural world as constituted by the Romans—*ager* for cultivation, *saltus* for grazing, and *silva* for woodlands and forest—the first two of these, *ager* and *saltus*, would have seriously infringed upon the third—upon *silvus*, that is—by the end of antiquity. In that light, one can only consider the Dark Ages that ensued as a reprieve for the forests of southern France. What with the collapse of any form of central authority, the dissolution of the great estates, and the virtual disappearance of all but the most local crafts and trades, the forests—

for at least five centuries—could regenerate. How much of early medieval folklore—whether in its tales or its iconography—draws, indeed, from the imagery of those wooded expanses. Dark, mysterious, often terrifying, those vast overhead canopies would represent, for large parts of a population in flight, refuge itself. The early Christian *foresta*, by now, had come to replace the Gallo-Roman *urbanitas*.

The invisible veil that falls between the cultivated and the uncultivated, "that interface between *cultum* and *incultum*," as Aline Durand describes it in her luminous work *Les paysages médiévaux du Languedoc*, serves to delineate anthropic space from the surrounding sylvatic.[2] It draws the line between what's ours and what isn't. One discovers that this veil, this interface, begins receding—once again—with the Carolingian. In fact, as the living conditions in society begin to improve *at any given moment in history*, that reclamation of natural space, infallibly, resumes. Indeed, the first wave of medieval clearings—that of the ninth century—might be considered comparable to those in antiquity. If it reduced the total surface of the forest floor, it did nothing, on the other hand, to transform the biological nature of the forest itself. It was simply incursive.

By the turn of the millennium, however, this condition had radically changed. "The threshold of the year 1000 serves as a virtually irreparable cleavage in the history of the Languedocian environment."[3] At that particularly flourishing moment for an emergent society, rife with a resuscitated faith in existence, a second wave of deforestation will affect the *silva* as never before. Under an ever-growing demographic pressure, new settlements—castral agglomerations and outlying *bastida* (fortified domains)—will proliferate across the landscape. Each, in turn, will encroach progressively upon the surrounding forest. Be it for the sake of extending pastureland, fueling the fires of a thriving *artisanat*, or heating households, this proliferation will cause—at a radiant moment in the history of humanity—irreparable damage to the forest floor. "These two waves of medieval deforestation will especially disturb the biological equilibrium of vegetal formations. In eradicating a large part of the *silva* itself, they will alter the very profile, structure, and distribution of the forest cover."[4] Inexorably, that cover goes on retracting. It does so, however, not only by diminishing in size but by changing in character. From an essentially mesophytic milieu—one in which plant life thrives upon a moderate degree of moisture—it finds itself more and more invaded by the xerophytic—one adapted to a limited amount of moisture. Here, anthropic and climatic forces will conspire to transform the environment of the entire region in an irreversible manner.

In the process, a new flora comes to predominate. That essentially mesophytic landscape gives way, bit by bit, to one dominated by orchards, vineyards, and woods cultivated for their usefulness, such as willow, fig, osier. By the end of the twelfth century, pomegranate, medlar, and black mulberry will add themselves to the growing list. Nothing, however, serves as a more accurate index to this emergent, anthropogenic environment than the incursion of the evergreen holm oak upon the deciduous *Quercus pubescens*. As the former begins to dominate the latter, the "forest primeval"— that vast prehistoric canopy—beats a slow yet inexorable retreat toward the most isolated (least populated) areas in the region. Not only deciduous oak but a whole variety of flora that had thrived at relatively low altitudes since the last glaciation (circa 30,000 B.C.) begins retracting, now, into the hinterlands. That

flora will find itself, soon enough, confined to the most remote—
usually most elevated—regions, restricted to some arboreal refuge
that is likewise subject to continual retraction.

Such massive paleofloral migrations are being traced by historians today. As a means of complementing their pollen and charcoal
analyses, these historians turn occasionally to textual and carto-
graphical sources, often medieval ones. Their readings—semantic
by nature—help confirm the data they've already drawn from the
field. Here, word comes to substantiate substance. For just as the
flora has left its ghostly imprint embedded in so much fossilized
matter, so, too, its memory has been sprinkled across the surface
of innumerable church cartularies, bullaria, monastic records;
been buried within the archival wealth of countless wills and tes-
taments, marriage contracts, notarized deeds; or, occasionally, been
inscribed across the surface of cadastral survey maps, outlining
the limits of given properties. Within such documents, a stray
phytotoponym—an oblique reference, say, to some olive grove
offered up as part of a medieval dowry—gives researchers, on occasion, an invaluable aperçu of the floral environment of a particular locale at a given historical moment.

Fagus sylvatica, or common beech, is a perfect example in point.
For the expanse that that tree once occupied can still be measured
today, either by the lingering presence of ancient place-names in
current usage or by the detection of such names in medieval records. In toponymic form, the tree appears under a variety of syn-
onyms: *Fage, Fau, Fagette, Fageas, Fayard,* and so on. In each and
every case, these place-names testify to a vanished environment.
Infallibly, they indicate the exact location of forests that—in
retracting—have left nothing for memento but their own estranged
vocables. Among the many eloquent examples cited by Aline

Durand, one in particular—drawn from a medieval cartulary—refers to a certain *Faja oscura* located in the Causse du Larzac.[5] *Faja* signifies the tree itself, with all the nutritive oils inherent in its woody fruit, whereas *oscura* evokes the darkness, and thus the density, of those once-flourishing beeches. Long since converted into pastureland, that arboreal stand endures in a lone microtoponym: Lou Fagals.[6] Mnemonic marker, it designates little more than a tiny ramshackle hamlet in the *commune* of Les Rives (Hérault).

The word—along with its residual counterpart, the fossil—bears witness to those vanished landscapes. Properly interpreted, its seemingly inconsequential particles, buried in so much somnolent documentation, allow one a glimpse—at least—of that lost ecology. It's as if the word, as a token of human consciousness, had withstood the retraction and ultimate disappearance of that dense sylvatic canopy—that *Faja oscura*—in order to preserve the wood's very memory. Even more, *it serves to preserve our very own.* For in that retraction and ultimate disappearance, the interface between culture and nature—*cultum* and *incultum*—has vanished as well. Only the word, it would seem, has withstood that spoliation. Having done so, it reminds us of a time in which the woods—the earth itself—hadn't yet been sacrificed, alas, for the sake of ourselves alone.

Psalmodi

for Allen S. Weiss

No sooner is the name of that ruined Benedictine abbey, *Psalmodi*, mentioned than an image of monks chanting psalms in the coolness of some barrel-vaulted choir comes to mind. Sancta Maria Psalmodiensis, however, owes the origin of its name to something far different. Founded in the fifth century on an isolated mound (an *insula*, according to Church records) in the pestilent Languedocian marshlands, it had but one raison d'être: the extraction of salt from the immensely rich surrounding salt beds. It lay, indeed, as if aureoled in that most indispensable of minerals. If in Latin "salt" translates as *sal*, serving as prefix for a whole string of salt-extracting communities within the immediate area—Salses, Villesalse, Salières, Saliers, Salines, Salins, Salanque, and so on—in Provençal it translates as *sau*.[1] Drawing on that particular nominal, the toponym for this given area was originally Saumodi, not Psalmodi. It was far too tempting, however, for its founding monks not to make the phonetically slight but semantically massive transposition. A bit everywhere, early Christian scribes were evangelizing indigenous place-names, which invariably indicated some physical characteristic inherent to the place, in favor of some liturgical or hagiographic signifier. The spirit of the age—fervent, transcendent, transfigurative—was fixated upon the ascensional.

However ascensional, though, the monks at Psalmodi must have labored long and hard for at least four months of the year in those surrounding salt marshes. With the collapse of the Roman Empire, the Church, and especially its outlying monasteries, came to assure the continuity of that earliest littoral industry. Psalmodi itself had been constructed over the ruins of a Gallo-Roman villa where salt and the salting of perishables had constituted the principal sources of income. Altars to Jupiter and Silvanus, as well as a certain quantity of Gallo-Roman ceramics, attest to such a settlement. Now, though, the Church, as the only functioning socioeconomic structure in place, had come to monopolize—here as elsewhere—that precious commodity. It would do so, in fact, throughout the duration of the Dark Ages. From Barbio and Farli in Italy to Gerri de la Sale in Catalonia, monks were charged with the extraction of salt. They'd draw seawater through narrow canals *(graus)* into self-enclosed salt ponds. There, in evaporating basins *(partène-ments)*, the seawater would lose nine-tenths of its volume before being channeled into even narrower conduits *(aquilae)* that led, finally, to the shallowest basins of all *(aires salantes)*. Fully exposed to the evaporating agents of a relentless sun and a dry, violent wind (the *mistral*), the salt could at last be brought to a dehydrated state, raked into camel-backed mounds *(camelles)*, and prepared for transport.

One may read in the Life of Saint Hilarius how that fifth-century figure—who'd only travel by foot—walked thirty thousand paces from Arles to the salt flats below. There he encouraged the ecclesiastic workforce in their annual salt harvest and furthermore invented a device (an *automata*) for drawing water mechanically into the salt pans with the aid of paddle wheels. Nothing could illustrate more effectively the role of the Church in the salt industry at that particular time than this passing glimpse of an engaged cleric. Theory wedded to practice, a millennial labor in an essentially pestilent area—*inter mare et stagnum*—could now be considered a righteous task.

It was at this very time that Saumodi—by a subtle transposition in spelling—found its name changed to Psalmodi. This shift would represent the outset of what is now called the "ecclesiastic phase": a period in which the Church would monopolize the production and distribution not only of salt but of wine, grain, and oil—of most staple commodities, in fact. At Psalmodi, the earliest traces of a Christian community—sepulchers, funerary accessories, and the like—date from this period: namely, the fifth century. If in 721 marauding Saracens destroyed the original Merovingian church, designed according to a square floor plan with a barrel-vaulted semicircular apse, by 783 a second church with an adjoining cloister would replace it. By 815, the abbot of Psalmodi, a certain Théodomirus, could boast—in the course of a theological debate—of the presence of 140 resident monks. Psalmodi, in fact, had become one of the largest monasteries in all Europe. Its history, though, like that of any Dark Age community, would be filled with vicissitudes. Fleeing yet another Saracen attack in 909 *(per oppressionem paganorum)*, the monks took refuge in a fortified settlement nearby. It wouldn't be until

1004, however, in the presence of five officiating bishops, that the monastery was reconsecrated and could resume its former activities to the fullest. The Age of Invasions had at last ended. And, in the ensuing peace, as the populations of Europe doubled over the next two centuries, salt would become—in one historian's words—a "strategic product."[2]

Psalmodi, in such circumstances, could only prosper. Indeed, it prospered to such an extent throughout the twelfth century—coming to possess over ninety monasteries, priories, churches, and agrarian estates in an ever-expanding area—that it undertook the construction of a church of inordinate proportions. This construction would lead, ultimately, to Psalmodi's downfall. The church, Romanesque in its conception yet increasingly Gothic in its innovation (such as its elaborately groined vaulting), stood over seventy meters in length and thirty-five meters in width. Its walls were massive and its buttresses, imposing. In construction for over fifty years, and never—in fact—finally completed, it drove the monastery, by 1180, into deep financial difficulties, obliging the abbot to take out larger and larger loans while relinquishing, as collateral, more and more property. By 1203, massively indebted as the result of this pretentious construction, a victim of its own immodesty, Psalmodi had to place itself under the protectorship of Philippe Auguste, king of France. This loss of autonomy would lead, soon after, to the sale of Aigues-Mortes, a yet barren expanse of land at no more than five kilometers' distance that would serve, in 1248, as the point of embarkation for Saint Louis's Seventh Crusade. The monastic was falling—inexorably—into the hands of the political.

Psalmodi's history, henceforth, is one of unremitting decline. By the end of the thirteenth century, it had surrendered much of its autonomy to the bishop of Marseille, and by the end of the fifteenth, had even lost the power to elect its own abbot. Far worse, however, awaited this once prestigious community. By 1537, the monastery—having fallen into total neglect—was denied all ecclesiastic standing whatsoever and underwent secularization. Bereft, confused, its monks wandered off to nearby Aigues-Mortes, and the edifice itself—in the midst, now, of the Wars of Religion—became subject to an endless succession of pillaging parties.

It's at this time that a curious "slip" begins to appear in archival records in regard to that menaced structure. For its toponym underwent, once again, a perfectly slight but immensely revelatory transformation. Psalmodi, henceforth, found itself transcribed as *St. Maudi*. If the pronunciation of these two locatives is virtually identical, their value as signifiers couldn't be more antithetical. *Psalmodi* can only evoke psalms, psalmodic music, the plucking of string instruments, and the accompaniment of voices in a melodious state of devotion. *St. Maudi*, on the other hand, even if it obliquely refers to Saint Maud, a derivative of Saint Mathilda, draws on the French qualifier *maudit*: damnable, accursed. The vocable alone openly proclaims the doom—the malediction—that had befallen that once flourishing community.

What's in a name? One might well answer in this instance: everything. From the founding vocable, *Saumodi*, with its evocation of salt *(sau)* as the material determinant for the site itself, to its revelation—for a thousand years—as *Psalmodi*, only to evolve finally, into the self-deprecating *St. Maudi*, one has gone from substance (salt) to spirit (psalm), thence to that spirit's demise as a result of such compounded misfortune. "It took scarcely two thousand years," wrote one author referring not to the site but to

the surrounding environment, "to convert those once navigable
lagoons into pestilent swampland, annihilating age-old vegetation, transforming a gracious archipelago of green islands into an
arid wasteland, rendering this coastal network desperately arid
and implacably monotonous."[3] It took far less than two thousand
years, one might paraphrase, to see the underlying values of an
entire civilization—exemplified by such a place—rise out of inert
matter only to relapse, with time, into such desuetude. The very
mysteries that civilization had once come to celebrate had, by
now, undergone irreparable damage. As victim of its own pretentious ambitions—victim, too, of the gabelle, a crippling salt tax
imposed by the king on both producer and consumer alike, not to
mention the probable clogging of its canals and flooding of its salt
pans—Psalmodi, inexorably, went under. It would be set afire in
1704 by Calvinists and converted, soon after, into a public quarry.
Dismembered, its once majestic structure would be carted off
piecemeal into the surrounding countryside. *St. Maudi*, indeed.

In examining the evolution of a single, seemingly perfunctory
place-name, one might well have fallen, in fact, upon a paradigm
for an entire civilization drawn from three critical moments of its
existence. With scarcely any perceptible difference in pronunciation, these virtual homonyms—*Saumodi, Psalmodi, St. Maudi*—
come to decline themselves in a somber invocation of their own.[4]

The Fifth Element

From Manna to Exaction

that the gabell of salt shulde ron through the realme
Jean Froissart, *Chronicles*, trans.
John Bourchier, Lord Berners

"In the absence of ceramic containers," wrote Fernand Benoît, "it's difficult to trace the exact routes taken by the salt trade."[1] Ponderous, ungainly, salt was transported in bulk for the most part—on barges, flatbed wagons—or, once retailed, bundled in canvas sacks and dispatched on pack animals to its final destination. As testimonials to its passage, it wouldn't leave the kind of recipients—the ceramic jars and wooden kegs—as would wine and olive oil. To the contrary, it dissolved all too readily within the digestive tracts of humans and livestock alike, or it went to pickle meat and fish or tan hides in tanneries. This "fifth element," as it has frequently been called, was as evanescent as air itself. Utterly essential to existence, it left—curiously enough—little or no written record of its extraction, distribution, or consumption throughout the better part of the early Middle Ages. Occasionally, an episcopal charter *(chartula)* would attest to some donation such as that of Childebert, the son of Clovis, bequeathing salt ponds in the vicinity of Marseille to the Abbey of Saint Victor. For the most part, though, salt—that most staple of commodities—was passed over in silence. Throughout the Dark Ages, it remained a mute mineral. Because it was harvested and commercialized from the sixth to the eleventh centuries by monks in monasteries located directly alongside the salt ponds, this particular period in the salt trade has been classified as "ecclesiastic" (see the preceding essay). Extracted in modest quantities and distributed over small areas to scattered, relatively underpopulated communities, salt would lead—as an indispensable quantity—a surprisingly anonymous existence.

It has, however, certain unique characteristics. Only found in specific areas, salt can, by its very concentration, be easily overseen, controlled, monopolized. In heavy demand everywhere, it's only harvested in a limited number of microregions throughout the Mediterranean. Among those regions, the Languedocian coastline is particularly privileged. With the high salinity of its ponds naturally protected from the open sea by a bracelet of sandbars and the evaporative powers of both a radiant sun and a dry violent wind, the area combines all the conditions necessary for the exploitation of that essential mineral. In this sense, too, salt is particularly subject—as has already been suggested—to the monopolizing interest of its owners: the Church, in this instance.

A readily circumscribed source of considerable value, salt has been the coveted object of a closed economy since antiquity. One can assume, however—given the breakdown of the Roman Empire and the ensuing disorder throughout the early Middle

Ages—that the power of the monasteries in the salt trade, although absolute in principle, was relatively temperate in practice. One has to wait until the rise of feudalism in the late tenth century and what has been called the "domainal period" to discover a sudden, aggressive policy in regard to salt. It became subject, at this time, to substantial if irregular increases both in taxes and toll charges. A "nebula of feudal landlords," both secular and ecclesiastic, had come into possession of the salt basins, replacing the monasteries in an ever-growing monopoly over that critical substance.[2]

Given the sudden increases in both taxes and toll charges, one has, at last, a certain amount of archival record regarding that otherwise evanescent traffic. In fact, one soon realizes that the written history of salt is, essentially, that of the exactions and impositions, the fiscal penalties placed upon that general good for the personal benefit of a privileged few. There is next to no record, for instance, of how salt—that "God-given manna" in Sébastien Vauban's words—was once cultivated: how, that is, seawater was introduced, each spring, into the freshly prepared salt ponds, then channeled into the evaporating beds of the far shallower salt pans.[3] There, by late summer, it would be raked into pyramids and prepared for transport (fig. 22). Far more revealing, however, there is virtually no record whatsoever of those who harvested this indispensable mineral: the *paludiers*, or salt farmers, gathered in great numbers as a seasonal workforce between the wheat harvest in June and the grape harvest in September. In the midst of a paludal environment, under a remorseless sun that casts, in such surroundings, only its own blinding reflection, they'd toil all summer long in total anonymity for subsistence wages. That "God-given manna" had long since turned to common

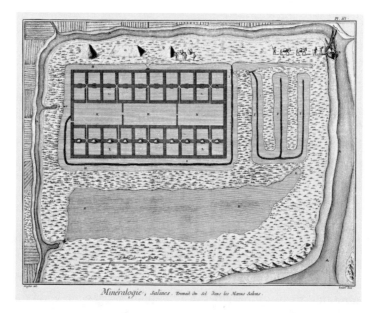

Minéralogie, Salines. Travail du sel dans les Marais Salins.

Figure 22. The process of preparing, harvesting, and transporting salt from the salt flats. Plate from Diderot and d'Alembert's *Encyclopédie*, 1768.

merchandise. It left no traces of itself except in the very first, relatively summary balance sheets kept by a growing number of commissioned agents.

By the early twelfth century, salt was coming increasingly under the control of so-called state monopolies. Great houses such as those of Toulouse and Aragon had begun replacing a plethora of lesser, aristocratic holdings, imposing as they did an ever more centralized—ever more efficient—system of taxation. By 1140 mention is made of an entirely new salt tax, the *salinum* or *salnaria*. Henceforth, salt will transit through state-established *sauneries* serving as both depots and clearinghouses. There, it will either be sold off by a new class of merchants—a substantial part of their profits going to the *domini salis*, the salt lords—or transit to yet other *sauneries* after having fallen subject to both a storage commission and a transit charge. Salt, of course, has always been taxed. But those taxes, for the most part, had been local, fluctuating from one place to the next, and never of a uniform nature. They'd be imposed, for instance, at river crossings or at the gates of certain cities at prescribed moments of the year. Now, however, as the great houses came to absorb the privileges of the scattered feudal estates, the salt tax became more and more standardized, generalized, absolute. By 1259, not only the *salinum* but a new "fiscal instrument of terrifying efficacity" would be imposed upon Provence by Philippe VI de Valois: the *gabelle*.[4] From the Arab *al kabala*, signifying tribute and, by inference, tax, both the word and the practice itself—one may safely assume—were introduced into the European economy by returning Crusaders. Now, salt would be taxed not merely in transit but at every phase of its existence. From its very points of extraction—the salt flats themselves—where it would be purchased in bulk by court-commissioned agents, to the most remote hawker in the hills, selling tiny satchels of that commodity out of his wheelbarrow, not a single transactional moment in that immensely complex process wouldn't fall subject, now, to that all-invasive regimen. The *gabelle*, suddenly, was everywhere, affecting everything, generating for the court more revenue than that collected on every other good and produce combined.

"The fiscality on salt . . . becomes part of the enlarged market economy of its times," writes Yves Grava. "The court calls upon financial experts *(techniciens de l'argent)* and tax farmers *(fermiers)* to advance the court large sums of money against pending receipts from the sale of salt."[5] It's at this very moment, too, that an army of accountants, bookkeepers, notarial clerks, not to mention the merchants themselves, begin recording, in the most meticulous detail, each and every pecuniary movement in the transactional life of salt. Now as never before one can trace that substance on a day-by-day basis, but only—it would seem—as a nondescript commodity from which immense profits could be wrung. Within the written record, its ability to nourish, to furnish indispensable minerals to humankind, to serve in a multitude of ways for the preservation of life-sustaining foodstuffs, goes unmentioned. To the contrary, it is always treated as something neutral, indeterminate, quantifiable but unqualifiable, from which those immense profits could be extracted. "The chandler *(grenetier)* and the assessor *(contrôleur)*," according to a royal enactment of 1377, "will record in their account books the exact quantity of salt to be found in the saltern *(grenier)*, the name of its owner, and the date of its deposit. In each saltern there will be three separate locks serviced by three separate keys. The registrar *(greffier)* will record both the date and specific quantities of the salt under transaction, and when the saltern is thoroughly empty, the chandler, the assessor, and the tradesman *(marchand)* will determine together the total sales thereof."[6]

Quite clearly, salt is no longer the dark mineral of the early Middle Ages. As profits rise, daily entries touching upon its commodification grow more and more explicit. An account book kept by an Italian salt merchant in the city of Avignon between the years 1376 and 1379 serves to illustrate the attention given to each discrete transaction. The subject of an elucidating study by Christiane Villain-Gandossi, this account book, bound in heavy parchment, contains no fewer than 124 densely inscribed folio pages on Fabriano rag paper (fig. 23). One of the most revealing aspects of this particular volume is the handwriting itself. Known as "Gothic mercantile cursive," this script is "characteristic of societies in which writing—grown indispensable, now, to every aspect of daily life—needed to be drafted rapidly since it was being employed in such a profuse manner. In short, it had to adapt itself to the pressing demands of a new commercial era."[7] Reading of that sociocultural acceleration, one finds oneself, today, on familiar grounds. For hasn't the present age undergone a massive acceleration of its own in which the written word has seen itself funneled—as if absorbed—into the foaming green particles of a new cursive, adapted, yet once again, "to the pressing demands of a new commercial era?"

This fourteenth-century ledger abounds with minutiae. Day after day, entry after entry, one can follow the commercialization of salt in elaborate detail from its point of inception: from the salt flats, with their assessors and salt farmers, their jobbers and bargemen, to the urban world of commercial brokers, notaries, and papal emissaries, not to mention a plethora of middlemen involved in the loading and unloading, the stockage and distribution of that precious commodity. Each of these figures, however, is only mentioned in terms of the profits and losses that each has incurred; the tolls, taxes, carrying charges for which each is liable. Indeed, in leafing through these pages, one has the unmistakable impression that it isn't salt—that ghostly mineral—that is being extracted but revenue. Salt itself only enters that "Gothic mercantile cursive"— ciphered, codified, ritualized—as an inexhaustible source of inexhaustible income.

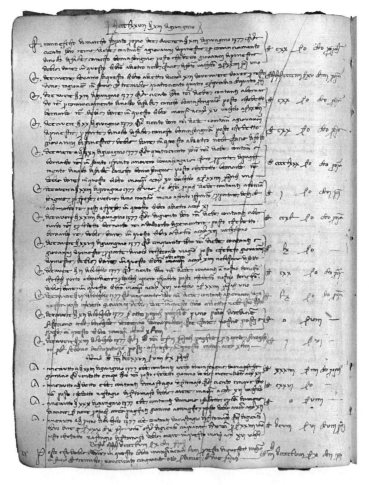

Figure 23. An example of Gothic mercantile cursive from the account book of Francesco Datini, barred after the account had been duly balanced. Archivio di Stato di Prato, Fondo Datini, no. 168, folio 14v. (Reproduced by kind permission of the Ministry of Cultural Heritage and Environmental Conservation.)

History is rarely more, in fact, than what history chooses to record. Often that choice, such as here, limits itself to some inexorable process of individual or collegial appropriation. It deals all too frequently with ends, end-products, the cumulative results of some entrepreneurial *mainmise*. Only what's "taken" is duly considered. Only what's extracted, duly valorized. Forgotten in that very process, though, is the wash of those high winter tides that would deposit—with unfailing regularity—that quintessential element over the salt ponds of southern France. Forgotten, that that gratuitous accretion of indispensable crystals had, in fact, been generated by nature and nature alone. That the "taken," with all its profits and privileges, had been nothing more than something that once was boundlessly—impartially—"given."

꧁

Mary Magdalene the Odoriferous

for Ann Willeford

> It is this that we call relics: something fallen under the imprint
> of a vibrant word.
>
> Saint Victricius of Rouen (†410)

I

Myths exist because they must. Gratifying deep-seated human
necessities, they come to illustrate otherwise obscure or suppressed regions of the psyche, and—so doing—provide those regions with a face, a figure, a scenography of their own. For centuries, for instance, the myth of Mary Magdalene's presence in
Provence brought solace to generations of miracle-seekers. Even
more than the memory of the thirty-seven years Mary Magdalene
was reputed to have spent doing penitence in La Grotte de la
Sainte-Baume, her face lacquered in an unremitting cataract of
tears and her naked body clothed in nothing more than her long

flowing hair, it was her bones—her venerated relics—that magnetized those generations of miracle-seekers. Often traveling barefoot over great distances, then entering the Basilica of Saint-Maximin on their knees, the pilgrims came for the relics alone. For only they could serve to substantiate the presence of that merciful figure; only they invest that radiant myth with verisimilitude.[1]

How, though, could so much fervor come to focus about something as stark, disconcerting, as a blackened skull or a few strands—reportedly—of her luxuriant hair? In examining every bit of available documentation touching upon those relics, and—by extension—the cult of Mary Magdalene in Provence, one might even ask: how could that fervor have reached such dramatic proportions, given that there is no evidence whatsoever in regard to the authenticity of those relics? To the contrary, everything within the historical record seems to attest to their falsification. In a dire attempt to adhere to the mythopoetics of Mary Magdalene's legend, medieval hagiographers were quick to attribute as hers the mortal remains of any number of anonymous individuals. Faith alone, it would seem, endowed those femurs, scapulae, ossicles, with overwhelming thaumaturgic powers.

Mary Magdalene's bones were invented (using that word in its original sense, designating—as it once did—"discovered," "revealed") on the night of December 9, 1279. Charles de Salerne, count of Provence and nephew to the king, Saint Louis, acting under what he himself called "divine inspiration" *(inspiratione divina)*, removed his cloak, and—with bare hands—began digging out the earth in the crypt of Saint-Maximin.[2] He did so, it should be noted, in the absence of any ecclesiastic personnel. Sweating profusely (*guttas accumulando guttis*), the count soon came upon the alleged tomb—a marble sarcophagus—of Mary Magdalene. Even before lifting its lid, he could clearly recognize this tomb as hers, for it emitted a rich perfumed scent. Whom else could it belong to but the myrrophore herself? Charles de Salerne found further proof on removing its lid, for there, sprouting forth from the cavity of the corpse's mouth, issued—in place of a tongue—a long green branch of fennel. Just as roses were said to bloom from the mouth of dead Adonis and wheat from that of dead Osiris, this aromatic plant "spoke" in the name of Mary Magdalene's sacred attribute: as, that is, the purveyor of unguents.

Yet another discovery awaited Charles de Salerne. Just over the left eye socket of that corpse, a tiny patch of living flesh still adhered to the skeletal frame. For the count of Provence, there could be little doubt: it was just there, at that precise point, that Christ, in admonishing Mary Magdalene never again to touch him (*noli me tangere*), had grazed her forehead with the tip of a finger, rendering, thus, that tiny patch with immortal life.

Two certificates of authenticity (*authentici*) were also discovered within the tomb, one on the night of the relic's invention, another—puzzlingly enough—a full five months later. Examined by specialists today, these certificates have proven to be little more than crude forgeries. At the time, however, they went to substantiate Charles de Salerne's miraculous discovery and enhance his reputation as an ardent defender of the faith both in the eyes of his own royal family and in those of the pope himself. Indeed, in 1295, when Charles de Salerne, now Charles II, was received by Boniface VIII in Rome, he brought with him nothing less than the alleged skull of Mary Magdalene lavishly ensconced in a reliquary of crystal and gold. The skull itself, however, lacked its lower jawbone from the time of its invention. The pope was quick to repair this all-too-evident lacuna. Ferreting through the crypt of Saint John Lateran, a basilica also reputed to possess a good part of Mary Magdalene's mortal remains, the pope's delegates—in that richly stocked ossuary—came up with a perfectly matching jawbone. Charles II could now return to France with a skull not only anatomically complete but blessed with the authenticating tags issued by the pope.

Already, the cult of Mary Magdalene at Saint-Maximin had begun to draw increasing numbers of pilgrims. A product, no doubt, of the "spontaneous generation" that followed upon the invention of her relics, crowds thronged the basilica not only on the saint's feast day, July 22, but throughout the year.[3] They were automatically granted indulgences by their very presence. Furthermore, an increasing number of those pilgrims, in search of some form of remission, underwent a miraculous experience within the immediate proximity of the saint's relics, be it the skull prominently displayed in its reliquary over the altarpiece, her long golden hair and the bones of her arms that could be contemplated in crystal ostensoria, or the remainder of her body lying in state within the Gallo-Roman sarcophagus in which Charles de Salerne was known to have discovered it.

In examining the sarcophagus itself (fig. 24), one is given an idea of the collective fervor to which Mary Magdalene's reputed remains were subject. Bits of that marble tomb have been chipped off by those who considered the coffin—by its sheer proximity to the bones—a magic property, while its flush surfaces have been rasped for whatever stone dust the fervent could garner. This "down feather," as it was called at the time, drunk in a concoction with wine or water, was said to alleviate the pain of childbirth for

Figure 24. Reputed tomb of Mary Magdalene in the Basilica of Saint-Maximin (Var), severely defaced by the fervent in their quest for relics. Photo by the author.

parturient mothers. Silk ribbons, wrapped about either the sarcophagus or the various reliquaries, were also said to produce very much the same effect.

Pilgrims, now, flocked not only to the basilica itself but to a grotto located along a mountain ridge fifteen kilometers to the southwest. Up until the twelfth century (1173, exactly) La Grotte de la Sainte-Baume hadn't yet received—in the ecclesiastical record—the denomination of *Sainte*. Called merely *Balma*, a Latin word of Celtic origin designating a grotto, it wasn't in any way associated with the cult of Mary Magdalene for the first millennium following her death. The grotto was nothing more, in fact, than a natural cavity, thirty meters deep, twenty-five meters wide, and eight meters high, its walls seeping with the waters of a natural spring: the perfect setting for what one historian has called a "hagiographic fabrication."[4] What's more, a phonetic amalgam gave credibility to that fabrication. For a priory on the plains directly beneath the grotto already existed by the name of Sancte Marie de Balma. This priory was repeatedly mentioned in ecclesiastic charters from the early twelfth century onward.

There is every good reason to believe that the vocable *balma*, in regard to the priory, didn't derive from the aforementioned *balma* of Celtic Latin origin but the Latin *balsamum:* the balm with which Mary Magdalene had become inseparably associated. To confound one with the other in an age of linguistic elasticity was—it might be said—ineluctable.

The legend of Mary Magdalene's penitential retreat in the mountains of Provence spread rapidly throughout the thirteenth century, and the invention of her bones at the end of that century gave material evidence—if any were needed—of her venerable presence in that area. The grotto in which she was reputed to have passed the last thirty-seven years of her life nourished, seven times a day, on celestial fare by a host of angels, became every bit as sacred a pilgrimage site as the crypt of Saint-Maximin itself. In 1339, Francesco Petrarca, after having visited the grotto during the season of Lent, wrote:

> For you, this site, these innumerable caverns out of which
> seep so much dark and abysmal water, far surpassed not only
> the gilded palaces of kings but all of life's greatest pleasures
> and earth's most bountiful harvests. Here, as a devoted re-
> cluse, stripped of all clothing but that of your hair, you con-
> fronted three times ten Decembers, impervious to the cold
> and devoid of all fear. And because of this, the love and hope
> that lay deeply embedded within your heart allayed all
> hunger, mitigated all cold, and rendered even your hard
> stone bed perfectly bearable.[5]

How, one might well ask today, could a cult of such propor-
tions, generating such a collective unequivocal fervor, have arisen out of so much idle rumor and deliberate falsification? How, in violating the everlasting sleep of some Gallo-Roman *memoria*,

could so much anonymous bone have been attributed to that of the blessed penitent herself? How, in short, could an invention of such overwhelming spiritual significance have been—quite simply—invented?

II

From the very outset, the figure of Mary Magdalene lent itself to ambivalence. Be it Mary of Magdela, the first to see Christ resuscitated; Mary of Bethany, sister of Lazarus and Martha; or the anonymous sinner who washed Christ's feet with her tears and dried them with her hair—she would remain venerated as three distinct individuals by the Eastern Orthodox Church and only become one and indivisible in the West toward the end of the sixth century. It was Gregory the Great who declared at that time: "She whom Luke called a sinner, whom John named as Mary, is also—we feel—the one whom Mark designated as having been healed of seven evil spirits."[6]

Already, one can see how freely—not to say opportunistically— early medieval hagiographers dealt with apostolic scripture. Whatever served some immediate proselytizing need was permanently adopted. However, it's only in examining documentary and archeological evidence, according to Monsignor Victor Saxer— the most scrupulous of Magdalenian scholars—that one can begin to establish the groundwork for some verifiable history. How, though, is this possible when even the scriptures themselves remain ambivalent, if not, on occasion, contradictory? What's more, how can Mary Magdalene's veritable relics be traced when they'd become—from the eleventh century onward—the phantasmagorical obsession of a collective fervor? When, that is, any human vestige could be attributed as hers by an endless succession of nobles and ecclesiastics, far more motivated by the acquisition of whatever would-be relics they might come upon than by the slightest regard for any sense of objective criteria?

Little wonder, then, that the bones of that saintly figure—she who'd died, most likely, a recluse in the Palestinian desert—allegedly arrived in Burgundian France several centuries later. How could this have happened? According to an account given in a miracle collection compiled by the monks of Vézelay soon after 1037, Mary Magdalene's relics came into their possession directly from Judea, thanks—they claimed—to an act of divine intervention. Given, however, that "this theologians' explanation failed to convince general opinion, they resorted," according to Monsignor Saxer, "to supposedly historic proofs by drawing up two successive accounts in regard to the translation [i.e., the transfer] of those relics."[7] These so-called accounts, one discovers, are filled with contradiction. If in one, Eudes, the abbé of Vézelay, dispatched his brother, Aleaune, and a monk by the name of Badilon, to plunder the tomb of Mary Magdalene situated, they claimed—for verisimilitude's sake—in the Provençal city of Arles, in yet another, Badilon, acting on his own initiative, would recuperate her relics from a tomb located, now, in Aix-en-Provence. In these twelfth-century hagiographies, the dates of 745 and 749 are given, quite indiscriminately, for what could only have been, after all, a single, albeit fictive, raid on a most singular funerary deposit.

Yet a third account from Vézelay would contradict the first two, and—quite unwittingly—lay the ground for what would soon become the predominant cult of Mary Magdalene in Provence. In this third account, her relics were recuperated from neither Arles nor Aix-en-Provence but from Saint-Maximin itself. This, of course, would be the version that finally "took" but in a most unexpected manner. Giving the lie to the Burgundian accounts, fraught with "extrapolations and paralogisms," it allowed the Provençal clergy to claim—for the first time—Mary Magdalene for their very own.[8] For the Provençaux now claimed that the Burgundians had looted the wrong sarcophagus and stolen the relics of some lesser saint, Sidoine, because the two saints' tombs had been deliberately exchanged (Mary Magdalene's in alabaster, Sidoine's in marble) as a protective measure, they purported, during a period of Islamic invasion.

One is witness, here, to a curious exercise in medieval hyperbole. The documentation, perfectly fallacious in itself, came to vivify—nonetheless—an altogether unquestioned and unquestionable repository of faith. It's as if the words therein served to "flesh" with authenticity any bone that any officiating figure happened upon, endowing it with a mystery that, in order to exist, only needed to be named. Language, here, came to predicate the sacredness of matter. One learns, for instance, that "the Magdalenian cult, having firmly rooted itself within Latin soil, began to develop in a primarily scriptural manner. It is only after the martyrologies and sacramentaries had been transcribed that crypts and relics began to appear as if so many stone monuments and shattered bits of sacred body could only have arisen—like Athena springing fully armed and helmeted from the mind of Zeus—out of the prayers and meditations of the early Middle Ages."[9]

Given that the rumor of Mary Magdalene's mortal remains within the crypt of Saint-Maximin already abounded, all Charles de Salerne needed to do on that December night in 1279 was remove his cloak and begin digging. The rest, indeed, would follow.

A series of hagiographic fictions, beginning in Burgundy, had already prepared the way for Charles's "invention." One dubious authentication after another, one deliberate falsification after the next, and the veritable cult of Mary Magdalene would root—permanently, now—within the subsoils of Provence.

III

There remains, though, yet another document that is well worth considering. Toward 1315, the third prior of the Saint-Maximin monastery, a certain Jean Gobi, compiled a miracle collection. Arranged according to the cures miraculously conferred upon no fewer than eighty-five individuals (from the deaf to the leprous, the sterile to the insane), the forty-six parchment folios of this collection provide startling evidence in regard to the cult of relics at this particular time.[10] Even if one can readily dismiss the more supernatural aspects of these accounts, one is left—nonetheless—with a wealth of material testifying to the efficacy of such cures. For the bones, it becomes apparent, actually *worked.* No matter how sham the attribution, they brought the fervor of the devout to an exact focus, materialized that fervor in allowing it to fixate on some skeletal section, and, so doing, provided an ostensible basis for each and every ascendant appeal.

Even more, perhaps, the bones also furnished the supplicant with a name—that of the saint herself—and, thereby, with the possibility of a verbal address. For "it's the address which determines the effectiveness of a given cure," writes Aline Rousselle in *Croire et guérir.* "In the cult of curative relics," she explains, "a name (that of the saint) and an event (that of the cure) come to coincide."[11] The pilgrim's attention was not only fixed upon a perceptible object—i.e., the venerable relic—but raised, in turn, by the vectorial power inherent within the vocable itself. "Bodies of saints," writes Rousselle, "had become the media for a transparent transmission."[12] They represented not only "something" but "someone," and that "someone" the merciful agent of an altogether miraculous response. In appealing to Mary Magdalene, the pilgrim entered—ipso facto—into a dialogue of sorts: verbal on one side, thaumaturgic on the other. The pernicious solitude into which that pilgrim (or a closely related kin) had fallen as a result of some given illness or inhibition was—at last—broken. He or she could enter, now, into a play of reciprocities in which the address alone would provoke—on certain privileged occasions— the desired response.

One need only examine the miracle collection for evidence of the efficacy of such addresses. In kissing the reliquary of Mary Magdalene's arm, for instance, a deaf man found his hearing instantaneously restored (miracle number 10). Or, for a woman who'd fallen suddenly dumb in the midst of the wheat harvest, her fellow workers—in supplication before that same reliquary—found their prayers mercifully answered (miracle number 39). The parents of a blind little girl would enjoy a similar gratification: in pleading all night for Mary Magdalene's intervention, they'd see their daughter's eyes flood—come dawn—with the day's radiance (miracle number 28). As a last example, one might consider a mad woman, locked and chained for over thirty years, suddenly sputtering in the midst of her uninterrupted delirium: "Blessed Mary Magdalene, save me" *(Beata Maria Magdalena, adjuva me)*, and finding, thereupon, her senses restored (miracle number 74).

Even if these phenomena are considered on an exclusively linguistic basis, the testimony is eloquent. For the bones, as suggested, provided a license of sorts for a given invocation. It matters little, in the last analysis, that those bones were nothing more, in fact, than the pathetic remains of some anonymous fourth-century personage. They served, nonetheless, the supplicant's most ardent needs. Instances in which fallacious means have been employed for the sake of gaining salutary ends abound throughout the history of humanity. Modern anthropology alone provides endless examples of similar practices. Such was commonly the case, it would seem, in the medieval. The relics spelled recourse. If they themselves furnished the all-credulous supplicant with the vocable for a transcendent address, the address, in turn, not only released but channeled an abundance of psychic energy well past the zone of personal affliction. It thus invoked yet a second space: a celestial "elsewhere" in which—by the bias of that very address—the individual might, at last, find relief.

No less an atheist than Sigmund Freud would attest to "the extraordinary increase in the neuroses since the power of religion has waned."[13] In the absence of that "elsewhere," the appeal to anything past the circumstantial could only, with time, deteriorate. The allegorical landscapes of the sacred could no longer illustrate the blind supplications of the devout, furnishing them—as they once did—with visions of the beatific. There where Mary Magdalene, robed in nothing more than her long flowing hair, had answered the urgent appeals of the ill and destitute, a monolithic rationality had emerged in place. Medicine would replace miracle; deductive reasoning, the underlying tenets of an ascendant faith. Thus, the breath—in its entreaties—would come to lose, ineluctably, its own most radiant mirror.

‿

The Death of Genesis

for Isabelle Dangas

Given the privilege of assisting at the restoration of two major medieval fresco panels, I depart from the book's geographical context in this concluding essay to touch upon the Poitou.

PART ONE: EXCAVATION

The fingers cross. Or, more exactly, the three fingers of one hand, pinching the narrow shaft of a scalpel or spatula, come to meet— at right angles—the index of the other. The index, here, serves as support, as cantilever, for the delicate operation in progress: lifting, prying free no fewer than five distinct layers of obliterating whitewash from a parish wall. Beneath, we know, lies the fresco: lies, dormant, the suppressed life of so much sacred, medieval iconography. The instrument—insistent—glitters. According to the angle or the pressure exerted on the blade, a nearly imperceptible segment of dry plaster flakes from the wall. Later, these detached segments will undergo analysis, and we'll learn that the five layers belong to five perfectly discrete moments in history: among them, as we might have suspected, are the Hundred Years' War and the Wars of Religion. At each of those moments, every effort must have been made to protect the frescoes from invading armies. Just like the reliquaries or the richly illuminated, heavily studded gospel books, the frescoes needed to be hidden, concealed. The magic inherent in all this holy image (acknowledged as much by the invading warrior as by the devout parishioner) needed to be camouflaged at all costs. With a quick coat of whitewash, the works went under, thus saved from iconoclastic obliteration.

Why five coats, though, we might ask? Did the whitewash—with time—grow thin, transparent? Did the pigments, after all those years, begin showing through? We might even ask ourselves whether *one* of those coats, quite possibly, couldn't be attributed to some irate band of Huguenots, intent on purifying the place of all such effigy—all such objects of idolatry. We'll never know, of course. We'll never need to know, perhaps. For what concerns us, here, aren't the successive acts of effacement but the singular act of revelation: the underlying frescoes themselves.

A world of angels, potentially, awaits the restorer. As we watch her fingers cross, over and over, in so many measured gestures, bringing the pressure of an instrument to bear on a particular square millimeter of wall space, we might be reminded, readily enough, of surgery: of some minor surgical intervention. Even more, though, the whole meticulous set of eliminatory gestures recalls archeology. It recalls some archeological excavation that's been reduced—in this instance—to minuscule proportions. For we're dealing, here, with infinitesimal strata: with the tiny laminated deposits that have been left at specific moments in human history. Like the archeologist, the restorer goes under, works her way through a series of superimposed levels. Each of those levels, bearing witness to its own "specific moment," is given, of course, due treatment as documentary evidence. But it's the angels, the prophets, the kneeling donors, buried deep beneath so many obfuscating layers, that the restorer works toward. We watch her, now, as she pries loose—delicately as a goldsmith—flake after flake, level after level of dry, pulverescent whitewash.

One might think—at the very same moment—of one's own embedded deposits: of all the psychic effluvia that have accumulated through the years in the form of suppressed memory, obliterated event: in the crust that's formed, at successive levels, between oneself and one's own buried history. For we, too, harbor frescoes. Within each of us, murals of a private mythology lie hidden at a depth that only our dreams or, occasionally, our finest intuitions, attain. Gardens, stairways, faces full of innate beauty—of sudden, inexplicable terror, as well—seemingly swim at those inaccessible depths: swim, writhe, erupt in brief riots of pure vivification, driven by the rhythms—the archaic rhythms—of our first, founding experiences. Over them, of course, lie our own forms of whitewash, our own eradicating agents. Call them whatever one will—suppressions, inhibitions—they lie, like the whitewash itself, static, inanimate. They're not endowed with rhythm because, as incrustations, they're not endowed with life.

No wonder, one might find oneself thinking, that Freud often compared the mind—the psyche—to compressed, archeological strata. How often he himself visited Rome for the sake of observing the vast archeological operations in course in the early 1900s. For he'd found, lying before him—in the many excavated shelves of earth, abounding with workers and wheelbarrows—the perfect analogy for his own monumental exploration of the invisible world within.

We're not, however, in Rome but in a small parish church in the Poitou: Notre-Dame d'Antigny. Witnesses to another form of excavation, we watch the work unfold. Not only spatula, scalpel and, occasionally, lancet are being employed, but sterile compresses as well. The compresses, soaked in either water or alcohol and applied to the particular section of wall undergoing *dégagement*, help to soften the hard, desiccated layers beneath. It might, indeed, take weeks before a shoulder, a sandal, the slightest fold of a flowing, ochre red garment begins showing through. Bit by bit, though, in worked sections no greater than ten centimeters square, the composition, gradually, comes clear. Out of so many scoured partitions, it appears—*reappears*—entire. After at least five centuries of total obscurity, freed at last of every obfuscated layer, the work—once again—unfolds.

The scene before us, we discover, is that of the Pentecost: the gift of tongues. More, perhaps, than any other episode in the scriptures, the subject is one of dissemination: the promulgation of the Word. We've fallen, quite literally, upon a moment of pure radiance, for rays of light in deep sepia burst—fanlike—from a now nearly illegible dove overhead: the Holy Spirit. The rays, curiously enough, alight upon the eyes, not the lips, of the marveling apostles. For it's *vision*, we're led to understand, that has just endowed them with *speech*, the power to proselytize in all languages. Sight, here, as if antedates sound. The apostles, stunned by the magnitude of the gift, stand there, their gaze, the red stubble of their beards, their radiant haloes, lifted upward. They're flanked, on either side, by tall stalks of lilies. The petals of these lilies, we note, lie open like receptacles. They, too, as beneficiaries of this privileged moment, seem to be receiving—in that very instant—that same overwhelming luminosity from above.

What we are observing, here, consists of a laminated surface far less than a millimeter thick: the width, say, of an eggshell or a standard sheet of typewriting paper. What we are observing, indeed, resides in the incredible fragility of a near-negligible quantity: the flake-thin tissue of the fresco itself. And yet, on that surface, little thicker than the breath we'd blow over a bathroom mirror, the Pentecostal imagery radiates. The lilies in their spread chalices flourish. Is the bed of our own memory, we might ask ourselves, any thicker? Are the evanescent screens on which our dreams, desires, hallucinatory figurations, lie projected any *more* substantial? Different as the materials depicted might be, aren't we always—in fact—dealing with precarious supports? Ephemeral surfaces?

PART TWO: VISIONS OF
THE PENULTIMATE

It's the eyes, we're told, that vanish first: the eyes, the brows, the dark little apostrophes of the nostrils. For it's these—the delicate features belonging to each individual physiognomy, applied last in the fresco painter's diurnal race against the drying plaster—that "take" least. Unlike the broad, loosely rendered expanses of sky, of landscape and rich flowing garments, the features—to the contrary—go on, most often, at day's end nearly dry. And that fusional process called carbonization in which the pigments as if wed, inseparable, with the milk of the still unctuous lime, never occurs. The pupils, with time, flake from the wall, leaving little more than so many blind white orbits staring—rather desolately—into a landscape rife with miracle.

We're no longer at Notre-Dame d'Antigny, now, but in the low, cradle-vaulted crypt of Saint-Savin. Here, the problems of restoration are altogether different. For at Saint-Savin, it's not a question of removing successive coats of whitewash from the fresco itself, but protecting the pictorial surface from deteriorations arising from *within*. The problems here are organic, one might say, rather than superficial. The abbey, located immediately alongside the River Gartempe, is subject to seasonal flooding, and nowhere more so than in its subterranean crypt. Highly sophisticated studies have been made by the Laboratoire de Recherche des Monuments Historiques to determine the effect of these floodings on the locale. In fact, every modern technological means available has been employed for the sake of preserving these frescoes—these frail, endangered membranes—from total deterioration.

Dampness, of course, is the first cause. Rising up from the foundations below, it conveys not only its own saline particles but those it encounters en route. Upon reaching the thin, pellicular support of the frescoes, this dampness, in evaporating, will emit these particles in one of two ways. If the evaporation occurs on the surface of the wall, an "efflorescence"—composed of so much soluble material—will develop. This often takes the form of a "white veil." If, however, the surface proves to be sufficiently resistant, these same particles will be driven backward, where—inevitably—they'll disrupt the porous surface of some underlying layer. The "cryptoflorescence" of those particular deposits will, with time, undermine the frescoes from within, adding to the process of deterioration in course.

Once again, we watch her fingers cross. Watch the blades—the various surgical instruments—glint in the intense light of stage projectors. The projectors have been set at acute angles for the delicate operation in progress. This very moment, they're catching in their crosslight each and every particle of that rich Romanesque decor that she's in the midst of "stabilizing," if not restoring. The damage already done is considerable. Along with that caused by the saline particles alone (the desiccation of pigments and, just beneath, the "disadhesion" of the pictorial layer), humidity has brought a plethora of microorganic activity to the crypt. Each bacterial, fungal, actinomycelial colony needs to be treated according to its own separate properties. We watch, now, as sterile pads, soaked in streptomycin, are applied here; nylon brushes for removing algae, utilized there; blasts of compressed air driven into the wall's contaminated pores, a bit everywhere.

We're witnesses, really, to a rescue operation. For in the crypt of Saint-Savin, that masterpiece of visionary art, everything seems to have conspired to undermine and, ultimately, efface not only the frescoes but the very mysteries they depict. Low over our heads, on four successive registers, unfold the lives, supplications, and martyrdom of both Savinus and his brother, Cyprian. Through so many miraculous episodes, we watch them move, ineluctably, toward their fate. Nothing seems to stop these evangelizing brothers, either: tied to the rack, fed to the lions, even flayed to the bone, they travel on, undaunted. For here, we're being led across the landscapes of an unquestioned faith. Just beneath them run—in a steady, ongoing ribbon—the *tituli:* Latin inscriptions couched in rhyming distichs. These inscriptions once served to elucidate the various episodes to the privileged few (mostly ecclesiastics) literate enough to read them. Today, however, the problem isn't one of literacy but legibility. For the inscriptions, like the eyes, eyebrows, and nostrils, applied last onto a rapidly drying surface, have been the first to flake, deteriorate. Many have simply vanished. In one, however, we can still discern the words of an angel exhorting the brothers to travel as far as Gaul, where, it reads, "the recompense that God designated" awaits them. The "recompense," we're led to understand, is that of their glorious death as martyrs.

This inscription reminds us that the crypt itself was once a martyrium. Here, the bones of these brothers (long since lost) lay for centuries in sarcophagi, or—quite possibly—within the locked little compartments of bejeweled reliquaries. Over them— over, that is, these objects of veneration—rose the low cradled vault with its rich iconography. More than merely illustrating the lives of these saintly figures, the frescoes must have served to vivify their very bones, animate the sacred presence of their brittle remainders. Yes, far more than mere illustration, the frescoes— we may safely assume—were seen as radiant manifestations of the relics themselves.

How can we, as latecomers, even begin to appreciate this distinction, to measure the immeasurable mystery of such works? For our own vision is almost always based on cultural—aesthetic— criteria. We examine the frescoes in the crypt of Saint-Savin, for example, as "works of art," as if art and artistic proficiency alone could account for such power, such consummate expressiveness. It's not art, though, that informs the artist—we must realize—but something far deeper. Far earlier. Here, as elsewhere, a work of art is never more than a moment of highly concentrated vision that arose—goes on arising—out of a particular fervor, religious or not. And it's just this: the fervor itself that we can't imagine, measure, restitute. Fervor of the artist, certainly, but also that of an entire epoch—in this case, the charged mysticism of the Romanesque. How, for example, can we begin to reconstitute a world in which a nail, a splinter, a knuckle bone floating in the oil of some crystal reliquary once served as the point of emanation for an entire faith? For here, in the cult of its relics, the Church was founded (see "Relics: *Membra Martyrum* as Living Current," p. 35 above). In these low-hovering crypts, in these womblike chambers where the bones of its martyrs gestated eternally, the Church asserted its mysteries.

Wasn't it this, in fact, that brought them by the thousands, traveling at their own risk and peril over immense distances? Wasn't it this that drew the pilgrims not to the splendors of the choir above but to the bones below? For that is where, as Georges Duby wrote, "everything most dynamic in religious practice converged." There, out of those low hunchbacked sanctuaries, "issued invisible forces beneficial to the spirit and palliative to the body. No pilgrim would have ever thought that the mysterious figures whose bones alone attested to their presence would deny their favors to those who'd journeyed so very far to reach them."[1]

The frescoes, rising arched over those mortal deposits, served to clothe the bones, endowing them with the flesh and garments of pictorial allusion. For the miracle-seekers, "crushed," as Duby put it, "in mystery and dominated by the unknown," the paintings must have appeared as some kind of magic lantern projection of the femurs themselves.[2] They not only furnished the bones with the running episodes of a mythology, they embodied that mythology in living pigment.

How, today, can we begin to evaluate that fervor, that mystery, those invisible forces at play in the production of such works? For what's at stake isn't so much the loss of a particular cycle of fresco paintings, no matter how great that loss might be, but the gradual deterioration and ultimate effacement of an outstanding instance of charismatic vision. *Charisma, charismatic:* even the words themselves have suffered attrition, effacement. They mean little more, now, than a certain magnetizing force found—occasionally—in certain exceptional individuals. They've become, in the interim, personal attributes. For what else can we refer to, today, aside from ourselves? In the absence of all mystery—the rationalization of all awe—we're left staring at one another in a world deprived of its deepest dimension.

Once, though, the walls glowed. Once, the effigies themselves were charged with the radiant presence of the effigiated. A mirror of swirling pigments came to meet the amazed gaze of the pilgrim. Here at Saint-Savin, in the precocious spring of the Western world, an art innocent of its own genius and infused with an unquestioned faith cast past itself the promissory figures of imminent redemption.

PART THREE: THE IRREPARABLE

They're there. One has to stand, though, on the top rung of a stepladder with the projectors, to either side, trained like klieg lights onto the small semicircular patch overhead. Even with a pair of specially adapted magnifying glasses, however, they're virtually impossible—at first—to detect. The projectors, rolled this way then that so that their floodlights might catch the slightest glint, touch—suddenly—on three, maybe four, minuscule crystals embedded in the wall's pocked surface. Small as they are, the crystals shimmer. Sparkle blue. We're gazing, in fact, at the very last material traces of a depicted heaven: what lies, still encrusted, within the gray ellipse of a faded celestial vault. The analogy, of course, is all too evident. The crystals, like grains of scattered salt, constitute little more, today, than the vestige—the near microscopic residue—of a lost metaphysic.

Analyzed as lapis lazuli, this mineral pigment, we learn, was imported in the twelfth century from Afghanistan, ground into powder, and then applied *a secco*. Far too fragile to withstand contact with the carbonic acids inherent in lime, it was spread—as thinly as possible—over a charcoal base. Unlike the sweeping ocherous outlines of the figures caught in the lime's living matrix, these depicted heavens never fully adhered.

So perhaps throughout the whole world of Romanesque fresco painting, it was the heavens that faded first: the thin azure tissue of so much celestial projection. With the loss of nearly every cold tone whatsoever—from malachite to indigo—how can we help but feel deprived, today, viewing these works? Abandoned to the warm sanguines and ochers of our own earthen element, how can we help but feel excluded from those faded landscapes, their raised visionary kingdoms?

There's worse, of course. Much medieval fresco painting has vanished altogether or left little more than the most evanescent traces. The causes are multiple: condensation, desiccation, not to mention direct acts of vandalism perpetrated by invading armies. Vibration alone, emanating out of an overhead organ or belfry, can accelerate the whole process of "disadhesion," causing the pictorial layer to detach, gradually, from its underlying support.

Even lightning, we learn, can discolor entire areas of a fresco if the pigments employed happened to have a lead base. Lightning-struck, the *blanc de plomb* (often found, for instance, in metallic decoration) will be transformed into plumbic acid, leaving—like stigmata—a black flamelike deposit. Indeed, we're witnesses to a slow but inexorable process of volatilization, taking place a bit everywhere. Within our lifetime, figures, foliage, the luminous blue landscapes of miraculous event—the emblems of a bimillennial mythology—have disappeared. Even here, at Saint-Savin, we needn't look further than the tribune, overhead. There, the aureoles of vanished angels lie about the eradicated surface of the fresco like abandoned hoops in the midst of some long-forgotten meadow.

From Notre-Dame d'Antigny to Saint-Savin, we've traveled *under*. From so many overlying coats of whitewash to panels subject to the agents of effacement from within, our stratigraphic itinerary leads us downward. There's deeper yet, however. As with the aureoles themselves, we're often left with nothing more than the final preparatory sketches, traced across a wall of freshly applied plaster. This intonaco, as it's called, belies a yet deeper level. For when it has suffered deterioration, we reach the last iconographic layer of all: the underlying outline on bare wall. Called the sinopia, it's executed, invariably, in bold strokes of red ocher and underlined—more often than not—in charcoal. Today, however, a sinopia might offer scarcely more than the vague tracings of some disembodied saint, floating—it would seem—across the exposed masonry. Or, barely legible, the cheek of Mary might be detected resting in *miséricorde* against the outstretched arm of her dead son. For here, we've entered into a

world of pictorial ghosts and doppelgängers, the wraiths—say—
of some sacred gathering in the penultimate moments of their
existence.

Well past all hope of restoration, these works gradually enter
into an oblivion of their own. Before vanishing altogether, however, they're photographed, traced to scale, rendered in water-
color: documented, that is, from every conceivable point of view
except—one might safely say—their own. In Paris, at the Musée
des Monuments Français, one may consult these documents as
well. One can easily spend entire days poring over the massed
computerized material touching upon any number of vanished
panels, eroded domes. What, though, about the original works
themselves? The fresh rendering of so much miracle, so much
transcendent event? We're the heirs, it would seem, to an ever-
expanding inventory of effacements. Quite apart from the inherent loss of all that imagery in terms of its immediate aesthetic, even liturgical, value, what's at stake, here, is reference
itself: a pictorial mirror to our own otherwise inarticulated mysteries. Be it biblical, apocryphal, or hagiographic, Romanesque
fresco painting offered—for over eight centuries—a readily
available set of visual counterparts to those mysteries. Meta-
phoric projections of a metonymical existence, the frescoes rendered awe, adoration, and terror itself visible in so many running programs. They transformed our darkest emotions into
luminous myth, offering—as they did—vivid effigy in the place
of turbid shadow.

We might have traveled northward, gone as far as Château-
Gontier, for instance, where one of the greatest cycles of me-
dieval fresco paintings has totally vanished. The cycle, depicting
Genesis in a series of rich episodes, has long since flaked from

its high overhanging nave. We might have traveled there, nonetheless, simply for the sake of becoming assiduous witnesses to such a resolute effacement. We might have stared, indeed, at so much blank plaster as if the plaster itself, rather than ourselves, had undergone some irreparable form of amnesia—or worse. In fact, the paintings, depicting humankind's first instigating moments on earth, have suffered a death of sorts: that of an elevated, most particular, perfectly inimitable interpretation of Genesis.

The loss of any creative work of major semiotic proportions implies—ipso facto—the loss of the subject depicted. Along with the sign vanishes the signified. We're left, finally, with what remains: a world in which reference to the *other*, to *otherness*, grows—with each year—increasingly rarefied. Bit by bit, the depths into which we once gazed for the sake of encountering our own most sublimated identities crumble, flake, decompose. Wasn't this what kept us, in fact, at Saint-Savin? Kept us on the last rung of the stepladder, turning our head this way and that, attempting to catch glimpses of those last residual deposits—those near microscopic grains of lapis lazuli, glittering occasionally out of the depths of their pocked wall?

More, though, than the residual deposits—than the last lingering traces of some mineral pigment—wasn't it the image of heaven itself that we sought? The pictorial evidence of some divine captivation? Wasn't it, in the very last moments of the sign, the glory of the signified that kept us gazing into so much crumbled wall? Waiting for the gray—for only an instant—to glisten blue?

NOTES

Unless otherwise indicated, all translations from French are by the author.

APT: READING AN ANTIQUE CITY
AS PALIMPSEST

1. Here and throughout, I've drawn much of my factual information from Guy Barruol's two excellent studies, "Essai sur la topographie d'Apta Julia" and "Le Théâtre romain d'Apt," *Revue archéologique de la Narbonnaise* 1 (1968): 101–58, 159–200. I hereby wish to express my gratitude to M. Barruol for these two indispensable works.

2. "It would be interesting to determine the choice of such a site, subject as it is to the swelling and overflowing of a river capricious by nature, and to evaluate to what extent their interrelation has had a direct influence upon the structures themselves." Christian Markiewicz, "Prospection des caves d'Apt," *Archipal* 40 (Dec. 1996).

3. Barruol, "Topographie," 111.

4. Fernand Sauve, *Monographie de la ville d'Apt* (Apt, 1903), 81–82.

5. Barruol, "Topographie," 112.

6. Abbé Boze, *Histoire d'Apt* (Apt, 1813; rpt. Marseille, 1971), 103.

7. P. LeGrand, *Le sépulchre de Madame Saincte Anne* (Aix-en-Provence, 1605), 67; quoted by Barruol, "Théâtre," 160.

8. Quoted by Barruol, "Topographie," 123–24.

9. Abbé Giffon in his commentary on Abbé Boze's *Histoire d'Apt*; quoted by Barruol, "Topographie," 152.

DESOLATE TREASURE

The epigraph is from Aline Rousselle, *Croire et guérir*, © Librairie Arthème Fayard, 1990. Used by permission.

1. Silvain Gagnière and Jean Granier, "L'occupation des grottes du IIᵉ au Vᵉ siècle et les invasions germaniques dans la basse vallée du Rhône," in *Provence historique* 13 (1963): 225–39.

2. Jacques Le Goff, *La civilisation de l'Occident médiéval* (Paris: Flammarion, 1982), 14.

3. Yvon Thébert, "Nature des frontières de l'Empire romain: le cas germain," in *Frontières terrestres, frontières célestes dans l'antiquité* (Paris: Presses universitaires de Perpignan, 1995), 221.

4. Le Goff, *Civilisation*, 14.

5. Lucien Musset, *Les invasions: Les vagues germaniques* (Paris: Presses universitaires de France, 1969), 68.

6. Max Martin, "Wealth and Treasure in the West, Fourth to Seventh Century," in *The Transformation of the Roman World, A.D. 400–900*, ed. Leslie Webster and Michelle Brown (London: British Museum Press, 1997), 63.

CRYPTO-CHRISTIANITY:
THE SARCOPHAGI OF ARLES, I

1. Quoted by Fernand Benoît in *Les cimetières suburbains d'Arles dans l'antiquité chrétienne et au moyen âge*, Studi di antichità cristiana 9 (Vatican City, 1935), 2–3.

2. Henri-Irénée Marrou, *Décadence romaine ou antiquité tardive?* (Paris: Seuil, 1977), 45.

3. Jean-Pierre Sodini, s.v. "Olives," in *Late Antiquity: A Guide to the Postclassical World*, ed. G. W. Bowersock, Peter Brown, and Oleg Grabar (Cambridge, Mass.: Belknap Press, 1999), 619.

4. Paul-Albert Février, "La sculpture funéraire à Arles au IVᵉ et début du Vᵉ siècle," in *XXV corso di cultura sull'arte ravennate e bizantina: Ravenna, 5–15 Marzo 1978* (Ravenna: Girasole, 1978).

5. Henri Leclercq, *Dictionnaire d'archéologie chrétienne et de liturgie*, ed. Fernand Cabrol and Henri Leclercq, vol. 13, pt. 2 (Paris: Letouzey et Ane, 1937), col. 2291.

6. Ibid., vol. 12, pt. 2 (Paris: Letouzey et Ane, 1935), col. 2305.

TERRA SIGILLATA

1. See especially Jacqueline Rigoir, "Les sigillées paléochrétiennes grises et orangées," *Gallia* 26 (1968): 177–244.

2. Felix Oswald and T. Davies Pryce, *An Introduction to the Study of Terra Sigillata* (London: Longmans, Green & Company, 1920), 13.

3. Manfred Lurker, *The Gods and Symbols of Ancient Egypt* (London: Thames and Hudson, 1980), 94.

4. Henri Focillon, *L'art des sculpteurs romans* (Paris: Quadrige/ Presses Universitaires de France, 1964), 49.

5. Henri Focillon, *Art d'Occident* (Paris: Armand Colin, 1983), 16.

RELICS: MEMBRA MARTYRUM AS LIVING CURRENT

The epigraph is from Henri-Irénée Marrou, *Décadence romaine ou Antiquité tardive?: IIIᵉ–VIᵉ siècle* (Paris: Seuil, 1977). Used by permission.

1. Saint Victricius, *De Laude Sanctorum*, quoted by Brigitte Beaujard, *Le culte des saints en Gaule* (Paris: Éditions du Cerf, 2000), 279.

2. Saint Victricius, *De Laude Sanctorum*, quoted by Beaujard (*Culte*, 43).

3. Saint Basil, quoted by Bernard Flusin, s.v. "Martyrs," in *Late Antiquity: A Guide to the Postclassical World*, ed. G. W. Bowersock, Peter Brown, Oleg Grabar (Cambridge, Mass.: Belknap Press, 1999), 568.

4. Beaujard, *Culte*, 335.

5. Ibid., 278.

6. Ibid., 283.

7. Raymond Van Dam, s.v. "Relics," in *Late Antiquity*, ed. Bowersock et al., 667.

8. Beaujard, *Culte*, 370.

9. Saint Victricius, *De Laude Sanctorum*, quoted by Beaujard (*Culte*, 502).

10. Henri Leclercq, s.v. "Reliques et reliquaires," in *Dictionnaire d'archéologie chrétienne et de liturgie*, ed. Fernand Cabrol and Henri Leclercq, vol. 14, pt. 2 (Paris: Letouzey et Ane, 1940), col. 2302.

11. Béatrice Caseau, s.v. "Altars," in *Late Antiquity*, ed. Bowersock et al., 290.

VENUS DISFIGURED

1. Thomas F. Mathews, *The Clash of Gods*, rev. ed. (Princeton: Princeton University Press, 1999), 6.

2. Much of the material in the previous two paragraphs has been drawn from Émile Mâle's informative study *La fin du paganisme en Gaule* (Paris: Flammarion, 1962), 42–45.

3. Ibid., 44.

4. Brigitte Bourgeois, "La Vénus d'Arles ou les métamorphoses d'un marbre antique," in *CRBC (Conservation/restauration des biens culturels: Revue de l'ARAAFU)* 7 (1995).

5. Béatrice Caseau, s.v. "Sacred Landscapes," in *Late Antiquity: A Guide to the Postclassical World*, ed. G. W. Bowersock, Peter Brown, and Oleg Grabar (Cambridge: Mass.: Belknap Press, 1999), 21.

THE BLOSSOMING OF NUMBERS: THE BAPTISTERY AT RIEZ

1. Aline Rousselle, *Croire et guérir: La foi en Gaule dans l'Antiquité tardive* (Paris: Fayard, 1990), 197.

2. Annabel J. Wharton, s.v. "Baptisteries," in *Late Antiquity: A Guide to the Postclassical World*, ed. G. W. Bowersock, Peter Brown, and Oleg Grabar (Cambridge, Mass: Belknap Press, 1999), 332.

3. See Armen Khatchatrian, *Les baptistères paléochrétiens* (Paris: École pratique des Hautes Études, 1962).

4. Baptisms were originally celebrated only on the eve of Easter in the presence of an officiating bishop. Collective by nature, the service was almost exclusively for the benefit of adults intent upon conversion. Having previously "renounced Satan," and—by a laying on of the hands—undergone exorcism, the catechumens, segregated by sex, "went down into the baptismal pool in small groups, standing knee or waist deep, while water was poured on their head and shoulders or clerics, invoking the name of the Trinity, plunged them three times into the pool itself [emblematic of the three days Christ passed in the tomb]. Then, clothed in simple white garments and carrying lights, they reentered the assembly of believers, where they were anointed with chrism, embraced with the kiss of peace, and admitted for the first time to communion." Philip Rousseau, s.v. "Baptism," in *Late Antiquity: A Guide to the Postclassical World*, ed. G. W. Bowersock, Peter Brown, and Oleg Grabar (Cambridge: Mass.: Belknap Press, 1999), 330–31.

5. "Octachorum sanctos templum surrexit in usus/octagonus fons est munere dignus eo/hoc numero decuit sacri baptismati aulam surgere." Quoted by Maria Antonietta Crippa, "Aux origines de l'Église chrétienne, Ier–IIIe siècle," in Crippa et al., *L'art paléochrétien* (Saint-Léger-Vauban: Zodiaque, 1998), 67.

6. Émile Mâle, *La fin du paganisme en Gaule* (Paris: Flammarion, 1962), 223.

THE DELETION OF SHADOW:
THE SARCOPHAGI OF ARLES, II

1. Henri Focillon, *L'art des sculpteurs romans* (Paris: Presses Universitaires de France, 1988), 64.

2. Henri-Irénée Marrou, *Décadence romaine ou Antiquité tardive?* (Paris: Seuil, 1977), 49.

3. Cosmas Indicopleustes, *Christian Topography*, quoted by Marrou, *Décadence*, 98; my translation.

4. Jean-Pierre Caillet and Helmuth Nils Loose, *La Vie d'éternité* (Paris: Cerf, 1990), 124.

5. Ibid.

6. Georges Duby, *Art et société au moyen âge* (Paris: Seuil, 1997), 13.

7. See Anna Marguerite McCann, *Roman Sarcophagi in the Metropolitan Museum of Art* (New York: Metropolitan Museum of Art, 1978), 132.

CITY OF GOD

1. Jean-Pierre Caillet and Helmuth Nils Loose, *La Vie d'éternité* (Paris: Cerf, 1990), 83.

2. Jean Barruol, "Théopolis en Haute Provence et le drame de Dardanus," *Bulletin de la Société d'études des Hautes-Alpes*, 1975: 48.

3. Saint Augustine, *The City of God* 14.28.

4. Ibid., 22.30.

5. Jacques Le Goff, *L'Imaginaire médiéval* (Paris: Gallimard, 1985), 64. Le Goff here paraphrases the recluse Euches.

6. Ibid., 62. Le Goff here quotes Saint Paul.

7. Barruol, "Théopolis," 49.

8. Fernand Benoît, "La Crypte en triconque de Théopolis," *Rivista di Archeologia cristiana* 27 (1951): 87.

9. E. F. André, *La Théopolis de Provence et Notre-Dame de Dromon* (Aix-en-Provence: Nicot, 1883). The Abbé André drew his materials from a document in the departmental archives of Digne.

LAYING THE DRAGON LOW

1. François Mathieu, *La Vie admirable du bien-heureux Saint Véran, evesque de Cavaillon, patron de la ville et du discèse*, 1665 (in manuscript at the Bibliothèque de Carpentras).

2. Aline Rousselle, *Croire et guérir: La foi en Gaule dans l'Antiquité tardive* (Paris: Fayard, 1990), 227.

3. Caesarius of Arles quoted in ibid., 185.

4. Marcellus quoted in ibid., 85.

5. Tertullian quoted in Abbé J.-F. André, *Histoire de Saint Véran* (Paris: A. Pringuet, 1858), 24.

6. Pliny the Elder, *Naturalis Historia*, 8.229.

7. Saint Augustine, homily 37. My translation.

8. Several of the antique columns and capitals in the choir of the parish church of Fontaine-de-Vaucluse originated in the aforementioned *nymphaeum*.

9. Francesco Petrarca, *De Vita Solitaria* 2.10. My translation.

THE DARK AGES: A HISTORY OF OMISSIONS

1. Michel Fixot, "La Provence de Grégoire de Tours à l'an mille," in *La Provence des origines à l'an mil*, ed. Paul-Albert Février et al. (Rennes: Éditions Ouest-France, 1989), 444.

2. Maurice Agulhon and Noël Coulet, *Histoire de la Provence* (Paris: Presses Universitaires de France, 1987), 23–24.

3. Renée Doehaerd, *Le haut moyen âge occidental: Économies et sociétés* (Paris: Presses Universitaires de France, 1971), 138, 58, 59 (Glaber quote), 58 (*Annales* of Moselle quote).

4. Fixot, "Provence," 480.

5. Doehaerd, *Haut moyen âge*, 351.

6. In conversation with Dominique Carru, June 14, 2001.

7. Most of the materials from the foregoing paragraph were drawn from Michel Fixot, "Provence," 464.

8. Jacques Le Goff, *La civilisation de l'Occident médiéval* (Paris: Flammarion, 1982), 29.

9. Warwick Bray and David Trump, *The Penguin Dictionary of Archaeology* (New York: Penguin, 1982), 196.

10. Doehaerd, *Haut moyen âge*, 17.

THE BLUE TEARS OF SAINTE-MARTHE

1. Most of the material for the present essay is drawn from Danièle Foy's excellent study, *Le verre médiéval et son artisanat en France méditerranéenne* (Paris: CNRS, 2001). I wish to express my gratitude to Madame Foy for her assistance and her indispensable research in this area.

2. "There is a common characteristic to all glassware of the eighth century, whether it emanated from the necropolises of northern France or from sites in southern France, Italy, or North Africa: that characteristic is its bluish cast." Danièle Foy, "Le verre de la fin du IVe au VIIIe siècle en France méditerranéenne," in idem, *Le verre de l'Antiquité tardive et du haut moyen âge* (Guiry-en-Vexin: Musée archéologique départemental du Val d'Oise, 1995), 210.

THE BLIND ARCADE: REFLECTIONS
ON A CAROLINGIAN SARCOPHAGUS

The epigraph is from Marie-José Mondzain, *Image, icône, économie* (Paris: Seuil, 1996). Used by permission.

1. Jean-Pierre Caillet and Helmuth Nils Loose, *La vie d'éternité: La sculpture funéraire dans l'antiquité chrétienne* (Paris: Cerf, 1990), 107.

2. Yann Codou, "Quelques données sur les inhumations de l'Antiquité tardive et du moyen-âge dans la vallée d'Apt," *Association d'Histoire et d'Archéologie du Pays d'Apt* 12 (1986).

3. Thomas Aquinas, *Summa Theologica*, Quod. 1, ix, A4. My translation.

CELESTIAL PARADIGMS

1. Henri Focillon, *L'an mil* (Paris: Denoël, 1984), 84.
2. John Sharkey, *Celtic Mysteries* (New York: Thames & Hudson, 1979), 92.
3. Marie Durand-Lefebvre, *Art gallo-romain et sculpture romane* (Paris: G. Durassie, 1937), 74.

VAULTING THE NAVE

The epigraph is from Raymond Oursel, *Invention de l'architecture romane* (La Pierre-qui-Vire: Zodiaque, 1970). Used by permission.
1. Xavier Barral i Altet, *Le Monde roman* (Cologne: Benedikt Taschen Verlag, 1998), 24.
2. Guy Barruol, *Provence romane*, vol. 2 (La Pierre-qui-Vire: Zodiaque, 1981), 20; my translation.
3. John Fleming, Hugh Honour, and Nikolaus Pevsner, *The Penguin Dictionary of Architecture* (New York: Penguin, 1991), 268.
4. Barruol, *Provence romane*, English summary trans. Marie-Thérèse Blanchon and Paul Veyriras, 427–28.
5. Robert Saint-Jean et al., *Languedoc roman: Le Languedoc méditerranéen*, English trans. Paul Veyriras and John P. Britz, 2d ed. (La Pierre-qui-Vire: Zodiaque, 1985), 384.

THE DOME: ARCHITECTURE AS ANTECEDENT

1. *Londres* in Saint-Martin-de-Londres derives from *Loudro*, which in Occitan signifies swamp, recalling the fact that this perched village, until the eleventh century, lay surrounded by marshland.
2. Robert Saint-Jean et al., *Languedoc roman: Le Languedoc méditerranéen*, trans. Paul Veyriras and John P. Britz (La Pierre-qui-Vire: Zodiaque, 1975), 387.
3. Henri Focillon, *Art d'Occident* (Paris: Armand Colin, 1983), 53–54.

4. André Grabar, *L'art de la fin de l'Antiquité et du moyen âge* (Paris: Collège de France, 1968), 34.

5. Ibid., 44.

6. Ibid., 49.

CLASSICAL ROOTS, EVANGELICAL BRANCHES

1. Victor Lassalle, *L'influence antique dans l'art roman provençal* (Paris: Boccard, 1983), 120.

2. William Alexander McClung, *The Architecture of Paradise: Survivals of Eden and Jerusalem* (Berkeley: University of California Press, 1983), 69.

3. Lassalle, *L'influence antique*, 21.

4. Alan Borg, *Architectural Sculpture in Romanesque Provence* (Oxford: Clarendon Press, 1972), 29, 30.

5. Whitney S. Stoddard, *The Façade of Saint-Gilles-du-Gard: Its Influence on French Sculpture* (Middletown, Conn.: Wesleyan University Press, Middletown, 1973), 19.

6. Borg, *Architectural Sculpture*, 81.

7. Stoddard, *Saint-Gilles-du-Gard*, 90.

VANISHED SCAFFOLDS AND
THE STRUCTURES THEREOF

1. Giovanni Coppola, "L'échafaudage au moyen âge," in *archéologia*, no. 274 (December 1991), 35.

2. See Nicolas Reveyron, "Les Matériaux: Nature, marchés," in *L'échafaudage dans le chantier médiéval*, ouvrage collectif, Documents d'Archéologie en Rhône-Alpes 13 (Lyon: Service Régional de l'Archéologie, Lyon, 1996), 34. I have drawn much of the material for the present essay from this excellent study, and wish to express my gratitude to the authors who contributed to it.

INCASTELLAMENTO: PERCHING THE VILLAGE, I

1. Julius Caesar, *Commentaries on the Gallic War,* quoted by Jean Barruol, "L'évolution de l'habitat dans les anciens évêchés de Sisteron et d'Apt," *Provence historique* 21 (1971): 316.

2. Fernand Benoît, quoted in Barruol, "Évolution," 318.

3. The term *incastellamento,* signifying "encastlement," was originally coined by the French historian Pierre Toubert in his study of that critical movement, *Les structures du Latium médiéval* (Rome: École française de Rome, 1973).

INCASTELLAMENTO: PERCHING THE VILLAGE, II (THE *CIRCULADES* OF LANGUEDOC)

1. Robert Fossier, "Villages et villageois," in *Villages et villageois au moyen âge* (Paris: Publications de la Sorbonne, 1992), 207–14, quoted by Aline Durand, *Les paysages médiévaux du Languedoc (X^e–XIIe siècles)* (Toulouse: Presses Universitaires du Mirail, 1998), 154.

2. Durand, *Paysages médiévaux,* 122.

3. Monique Bourin-Derruau, *Villages médiévaux en Bas-Languedoc: Genèse d'une sociabilité, X^e–XIVe siècle* (Paris: L'Harmattan, 1987).

4. William Alexander McClung, *The Architecture of Paradise: Survivals of Eden and Jerusalem* (Berkeley: University of California Press, 1983), 61.

5. Aline Durand, *Paysages médiévaux,* 244.

FAJA OSCURA

The epigraph is from Aline Durand, *Les paysages médiévaux du Languedoc (X^e–XIIe siècles)* (Toulouse: Presses Universitaires du Mirail, 1998). Used by permission.

1. Jérôme Bonhôtre, cited by Aline Durand, *Les paysages médiévaux du Languedoc (X^e–XIIe siècles)* (Toulouse: Presses Universitaires du Mirail, 1998), 183. Throughout this essay, I have drawn virtually all my materials

from Madame Durand's immensely rich, pluridisciplinary examination of the Languedocian paleoenvironment. I take this opportunity to express my profound gratitude for her exemplary work.

2. Durand, *Paysages médiévaux*, 301.

3. Ibid., 244.

4. Ibid., 210.

5. Ibid., 234.

6. I wish to thank Maïté Barascut, secretary at the town hall of Les Rives, for helping me locate *Faja oscura* (Lou Fagals) on the township's cadastral plan.

PSALMODI

1. Fernand Benoît, "Les abbayes du sel: L'héritage antique du delta au moyen-âge," in *Delta: Revue économique et littéraire du delta du Rhône* 3 (1961): 17–32. I have drawn a good deal of my information from this invaluable essay, both on the toponymy of the region in general and on Psalmodi in particular.

2. Gilbert Dunoyer de Segonzac, *Les chemins du sel* (Paris: Gallimard, 1991), 67.

3. Charles Lenthéric, *Les villes mortes du Golfe du Lion* (Paris, 1876), cited by Jean Pauc, *Les étangs à l'époque médiévale* (Lattes: Musée archéologique de Lattes, 1986), 151.

4. Today the toponym *Psalmodi* has been reclaimed from its illustrious past. A sun-bleached road sign to that effect leads one toward a sprawling Languedocian farmhouse flanked, on one side, by greenhouses for the year-round cultivation of chrysanthemums and, on the other, by the ruins of the abbey itself. Under excavation since 1972 by a team of American archeologists headed by Whitney S. Stoddard of Williams College, the ruins of the two pre-Romanesque churches and those of its immense Romano-Gothic overlay have left nothing in elevation except—symbolically enough—a beautifully keyed spiral staircase in limestone. This staircase rises fifteen meters up the side of an adjoining farmhouse and is occupied, throughout the year, by little more than a bevy of wild pigeons.

THE FIFTH ELEMENT: FROM MANNA TO EXACTION

1. Fernand Benoît, *Recherches sur l'hellénisation du Midi de la Gaule* (Marseille: Lafitte Reprints, 1980), 203.

2. Yves Grava, "La fiscalité du sel: Pouvoir et société en Provence au XIVᵉ siècle, La Gabelle de Berre," in *Le sel et son histoire: Actes du colloque de l'Association interuniversitaire de l'Est, Nancy, 1–3 octobre 1979* (Nancy: Publications Université Nancy II, 1981), 237.

3. Sébastien Le Prestre de Vauban, *Projet d'une Dixme royale* (n.p.: 1708, 102), cited by Christiane Villain-Gandossi, *Comptes du sel* (Paris: Éditions Bibliothèque Nationale, 1969), 81–82.

4. Gilbert Dunoyer de Segonzac, *Les chemins du sel* (Paris: Gallimard, 1991), 90.

5. Grava, "Fiscalité," 234.

6. *Ordonnances des rois de France* 4: 694, cited by Villain-Gandossi, *Comptes*, 81–82.

7. Henri Pirenne, "L'instruction des marchands au moyen âge," in *Annales d'histoire économique et sociale* 1 (1929): 18, cited by Villain-Gandossi, *Comptes*, 13.

MARY MAGDALENE THE ODORIFEROUS

This essay first appeared in *Verse* 19, nos. 1–2 (2002): 98–106.

1. In considering a particular relic, the pilgrim perceived not some isolated anatomical section but the holy body in all its integrity. "We cannot therefore deplore the fragmentation of relics," Saint Victricius would declare toward the end of the fourth century, "given that the sacred is not subject to diminishment. All can be found within each. There where a part exists, so does the totality." Quoted by Pierre Hadot in *Porphyre et Victorinus* (Paris: Études Augustiniennes, 1968), 63–65.

2. Monsignor Victor Saxer, *Origines du culte de Marie Madeleine en Occident* (Paris: Clavreuil, 1959), 235.

3. Ibid., 228.

4. Drawn from the title of Bernard Montagnes's essay: "Saint Max-

imin: Foyer de production hagiographique," in *Marie Madeleine dans la mystique, les arts et les lettres: Actes du colloque international, Avignon, 20–21–22 juillet 1988*, ed. Eve Duperray (Paris: Beauchesne, 1989), 49.

5. Francesco Petrarca, "Carmen de Beata Maria Magdalena," in *Poesie minori*, ed. Domenico Rossetti, vol. 3 (Milan: Società tipografica de' classici Italiani, 1834), 291. My translation.

6. Cited in Saxer, *Origines*, 3.

7. Monsignor Victor Saxer, "Le culte et la tradition de Sainte Marie-Madeleine en Provence," *Mémoires de l'Académie de Vaucluse* 6 (1985): 45.

8. Ibid., 44.

9. Saxer, *Origines*, 57.

10. This miracle collection is amply discussed in the above-mentioned essay by Bernard Montagnes.

11. Aline Rousselle, *Croire et guérir* (Paris: Fayard, 1990), 171.

12. Ibid., 243.

13. Sigmund Freud, "The Future Prospects of Psycho-Analytic Therapy," in *Collected Papers*, vol. 2 (London: Hogarth Press, 1950), cited by Rousselle, *Croire*, 129.

THE DEATH OF GENESIS

1. Georges Duby, *Le temps des cathédrales: L'art et la société, 980–1420* (Paris: Gallimard, 1976), 55, 67.

2. Ibid., 18.

INDEX

Page references in italic indicate illustrations.

Arles: barbaric invasions resisted
by, 20; depopulated by plague,
86; early Christian sarcophagi
in, 21–28, 22, 27; flourishing
of, 21; Saracen attacks on, 87
artifacts, digital representations
of, 3
ashlar, 127, 128
Ataulphus, 68
Atlantis, 158
Augustine of Hippo, Saint, 82,
158; *The City of God*, 69
Augustus, 7

Bacchus, 30
balsamum (balm of Mary Magdalene), 189
baptism: of children vs. adults, 57;
of Christ, 53, 57; for conver-
sion/rebirth, 54–55, 215n4
baptisteries: vs. baptismal fonts,
57; construction/plans of, 54,
55, 56, 57; vs. river baptisms,
52–54; symbolism of numbers
in, 54–55, 57–58
barrel vaults, 115, 117, 118, 126
Barruol, Guy, 11
Barruol, Jean, 73
Bartholomew, Saint, 131, *132*, 133
Basil, Saint, 37
basilicas, 114–15, 120, 124, 127–28
bas-reliefs: arcade decor on,
99–106, *101*; articulation/re-
semblance in, 129–31, *130*,
132; figuration of, 102, 105,
134; increased relief in, 134. *See
also* carved relief
bastida (fortified domains), 165–66
beech trees, 167–68
Benjamin, Walter, 3

Benoît, Fernand, 73, 74, 148, 175
Bible moralisée, 160
birch wood, 164
blanc de plomb, 207
Boniface VIII, pope, 186–87
Borg, Alan, 131
bories (stone shelters), xi, 147
Bram (Aude), *157*
brandea (remnants of martyrs'
clothing), 40
bronze: arrival of, 145, 164; coins,
15–19
Brunus, 130–31
Buoux, 147
Burckhardt, Jacob, 128
Burgundians, 78, 86–87, 90,
191–92
burial practices, 21, 72. *See also* sarcophagi; tombs
buttresses, 139

Caesar, 7, 146
Caesarius, bishop of Arles, 80
Calvinists, 174
capitularies, 85–86
cardo maximus (north-south
Roman thoroughfare), 6
Carolingians, 88, 90, 107
Carru, Dominique, 89
cartularies, 85–86
carved relief: on chancel barriers,
108, 109; shadows of/perspec-
tive in, 61–63, 102, 134. *See also*
bas-reliefs
Caseau, Béatrice, 50
castles *(castelli)*, 150, 151–52,
155–56, 159
Castor, 24
castra (fortresses), 149–50, 151,
154–58, *157*, 159

Text:	10/15 Janson
Display:	Janson
Compositor:	Binghamton Valley Composition
Indexer:	Carol Roberts
Printer/Binder:	Maple-Vail Book Manufacturing Group